The Gospel Stories of Jesus

Gospel Reflections for Year B

Mark

By Deacon Dick Folger

Illustrations by Kathy Ann Sullivan

The Gospel Stories of Jesus

Copyright © 2002

By Deacon Dick Folger

Published by

2339 Davis Avenue
Hayward, CA 94545-1111, U.S.A.
510-887-5656
www.folgergraphics.com
E-mail: dickfolger@aol.com

Printed in the United States of America

Library of Congress Control Number 2002094888
ISBN 0-9715211-1-5

How others have used
The Gospel Stories of Jesus

Jesus was a storyteller. And so we are all called to be storytellers for Jesus. In the closing words the Book of Matthew (28:19) we are commissioned: "Go then, to all peoples everywhere and make them my disciples!"

Sunday bulletins are great opportunities for telling Gospel stories. Our bulletin had been static for years. The front page had a picture of the church and just listed the Mass schedules and various parish phone numbers. It was the same week after week.

In an effort to make the front page of the bulletin more readable, we began printing my paraphrase of the weekly Gospel story. We included an illustration and a short reflection. We sent the *statistics* to page two. People seemed to like the stories, so I kept writing and by the time we had printed the full three-year cycle, I had written 152 stories.

The Gospel Stories of Jesus were next published in *Celebration*, the worship resource of *The National Catholic Reporter*. This gave the stories a national audience and a much wider use.

Many churches began to print them in their Sunday bulletins. At a church in Baton Rouge, LA they even read one of the Gospel stories at Sunday Mass.

A Franciscan priest wrote to say he found the stories "extremely helpful for me as I prepare for my Sunday homily." Another reader said "I love to read them on Monday and walk with the story or image for the week."

A jail chaplain in California wrote to say, "I find them a wonderful way to share the Gospel story with the inmates in Saturday chapel."

Bible study groups have used the stories as "meeting starters" and youth ministers say the kids like to hear these "mini-movies" of the Gospels.

This book is copyrighted, but readers are welcome to reprint the individual stories in church bulletins or other materials as needed. No written permission is required, providing the following copyright reference appears:
© The Gospel Stories of Jesus by Deacon Dick Folger.

Deacon Dick Folger

Table of Contents Year B

The Sundays of Ordinary Time

The Sundays of Advent and the Christmas Season

First Sunday of Advent
Mark 13: 33-37

You do not know the day or the hour...

The walls of Jerusalem rose like cliffs from the dark Kidron Valley. Across on the slopes, at their camp near the top of the Mount of Olives, Jesus and the disciples sat watching the shadows of evening slowly climb the fortress walls.

Below them, on the hillside, the Garden of Gethsemane had been swallowed into the quicksand of darkness. Only the weak light from one small campfire gave a faint tracing to the entrance of the garden's grotto.

Andrew sighed and leaned back against the trunk of one of the trees. "Looks like they're closing the gate over there," he said.

"Yes, I saw guards posted." Philip noted.

Jesus looked over at the two disciples, leaning on his right elbow: "Just as they will be on watch tonight, so must you Andrew and you Philip. Stay awake! You do not know when the appointed time will come."

Misunderstanding Jesus, Andrew asked, "Tonight? Should I stay awake all night?"

Jesus explained he was talking about a greater image, the coming of the Son of Man. The other disciples moved closer.

"It is like a man traveling abroad," Jesus began. "He leaves home and places his servants in charge, each with his own task; and he orders the man at the gate to watch with a sharp eye. Look around you! You do not know when the master of the house is coming, whether at dusk, at midnight, when the cock crows, or at early dawn."

"With so many thieves on the road at night," Andrew said, still missing the point, "the master would not likely travel at night. If he did, the guards would be caught by surprise."

Jesus smiled patiently and looked around at the others faces, then back

to Andrew. "That's an excellent point, Andrew," Jesus said, adding: "Do not let him come suddenly and catch you asleep."

No one said anything for a moment. They turned their attention back to the torches moving along the top of the walls of Jerusalem.

Jesus concluded: "What I say to you, I say to all: Be on guard!"

Our lives are lived on the edge. We are balanced between life and death. Anything could happen at any moment. Nothing could be truer than Jesus' words: "You do not know when the appointed time will come." We are left with this Gospel warning to be ready for the end of the world, remembering also the message of last week's Gospel: to love and care for one another is to love and care for Jesus.

Second Sunday of Advent
Mark I: 1-8

A prophet speaks

"Look, he's doing it again!"

The young man jabbed his friend with his elbow and pointed at the wild man standing waist-deep in the Jordan River.

An old man with a walking stick was wading toward him. When the river man lifted his arms in welcome, the wind caught his tangled black hair. It exploded into a lion-like mane. The wild man plunged the old man's head under water and the walking stick went floating away in the current.

Across the Jordan, on the other bank, dozens of onlookers were watching the spectacle.

The river man with the wild hair looked like a prophet, and many thought him to be one as well. He was wearing a piece of camel hide tied around his waist with a strap. Students of the law may have noted that clothes of camel hair were also worn by the great prophet Elijah.

"What is he doing, trying to drown that man?" the other youth asked. Another old man nearby heard the question and tried to explain..

"It is not a drowning, lad. The man is being washed clean. He is being purified so that he may become one of us Jews."

The three of them watched as the baptized man regained his footing and staggered to the river bank with John. Someone had retrieved the walking stick and gave it to the shivering old man.

At the edge of the water John lifted his arms again and shouted in exultation.

Someone called from the crowd. "Are you the prophet, the Messiah, the one who is to come?"

There was a silence. People waited, hearing only the peaceful sound of the river flowing by.

John's voice then rolled like thunder over the desert place: "The man who will come after me is much greater than I am. I am not good enough even to bend down and untie his sandals. I baptize you with water, but he will baptize you with the Holy Spirit."

A gust of hot wind filled their ears with its humming. When the wind dropped to a whisper all they could hear was the sound of the river chattering over the shallows.

Who is the prophet in your life? All of us have experienced someone who was like John the Baptist—someone who was a herald in the deserts of our lives. Was your prophet a family member, a friend? Perhaps it was someone speaking through the pages of a book. Possibly there were many prophets—a priest, a nun, deacon or brother. Whoever it was, remember them. They announced Jesus to you.

On this second Sunday of Advent we can recall that joy which filled our hearts when we first received the Good News that Jesus was truly in our midst and that he was baptizing us with the bright fire of the Holy Spirit.

Third Sunday of Advent
John 1: 6-8, 19-28

The voice
in the desert...

From higher up on the bank of the Jordan River, the crowd of curious people looked down at him. He was like a wild man, wrapped in camel skin. He sat alone on a rock at the river's edge. They stood a long time, watching and waiting.

John felt both warmth and cold. The morning sun was good on his back, chasing away the last chills of the night. His feet felt the cold water flowing over them. He stared down into the river flow, lost in thought about the one who was to come.

John's eyes were moist with emotion as he recalled the powerful revelation that God had bestowed on him that distant night ago. John remembered waking in the darkness to find the presence of God warm upon him.

The caress of the morning sun reminded him of the warmth that had filled him that night as the holy darkness resolved to dazzling clarity. Squinting into the astonishing brightness, John was filled with peace and understanding. He would announce the coming of the Light of Christ into this world. He would be the voice in the desert, crying out the good news of the one who was to come.

John stood up and turned to look up at the people on the river bank. The sunlight made a silhouette of the silent crowd looking back down on him. He knew they had their questions. Some were no doubt sent by the Pharisees to prod him with two-edged questions. He knew others thought he was a madman. John had seen their smirks before. He had heard their whispers and deriding laughter. Yet, John was filled with the power of God. The fiery spirit of God was upon him and in him and would soon stand before him in the waters of this very river.

From the water's edge he bellowed up at them: "Make straight the way of the Lord!" His words shattered the morning silence. John felt his heartbeat quicken as he stalked up the riverbank toward the crowd. He would make them believe!

✝

The Third Sunday of Advent used to be called "Gaudete Sunday" (Rejoice Sunday). It is truly a Sunday to rejoice in the news that John proclaims to the crowds. "There is one among you whom you do not recognize."

We, like John, are called to proclaim the coming also. We are invited to tell every one we know: "Rejoice! Rejoice greatly! Our Lord comes!"

Fourth Sunday of Advent
Luke 1: 26-38

Once upon a time in Nazareth

The first stars of the night twinkled down on the young girl. She clutched the hem of her apron and held it to her cheeks where the tears were still running. Her hands trembled. Her heart was pounding so hard in her throat she gasped to get enough air to breathe.

The man, a foreigner, had just vanished! He burst into nothing, disappearing in the blink of her eyes. Where he had once stood before her, there was now only the night sky.

But he had been there! Mary had seen him and he had spoken to her. His words echoed in her mind—strange words, telling her that God had chosen her…that she would give birth to a king…and that the kings' name was to be Jesus.

The striking image of the man was still fresh. His face had seemed to glow with its own light. Mary had been alone, taking her evening walk When she looked up she noticed him standing there on her footpath. He smiled at her and softly said, "Rejoice!"

Mary was still stopped where she was on the pathway, frozen in fear. She told herself to run, but she was. unable to move.

The peaceful silence that settled over Nazareth began to calm Mary. She realized she was not going to continue her walk. Nothing was ever going to be the same again. Still trembling she broke free and began to run back along the footpath that led to her house.

Mary burst through the open doorway almost running into Anna and Joachim who were lighting the lamp together. Anna looked up in surprise. "Back so soon?" she asked.

Mary could not speak. Her words caught in her throat and suddenly she was sobbing as her mother embraced her. Waves of unexplainable joy crashed like mighty echoes over Mary's heart.

"What is it, dear?" Anna asked as she stroked her daughter's long hair.

As if the sky would explain for her, Mary pointed out into the starry night. A bright star winked back and Mary knew it was the stranger. Yes, it was all true!

"Oh mother…" she began

Today, all these years later, we share the Annunciation again. We, like Mary, are called to believe. We are called to know it is all true. We are summoned by Gabriel, now, in our life and time, to rejoice! For unto us a Son will be given and the government shall be upon His shoulders and His name shall be called Wonderful, Counselor, The Mighty God, The Everlasting Father, The Prince of Peace.

Christmas
Luke 2: 1-14

The happiest night of the world

When the night sky began to streak with light, nine-year old Aachim scrambled on his hands and knees toward his sleeping flock. In the growing light the terrified shepherd boy huddled next to *Old Moto* as if his favorite sheep could protect him.

The dome of night looked like a pitcher of goatsmilk was being poured into its bowl. The whiteness spread like wispy clouds driven on strong wind. The pale light thickened and began forming into the shape of a woman with outstretched arms. Suddenly the milk-light snapped to life and an angel floated above Aachim. Her brilliant white robes billowed about her.

Aachim pressed harder against *Old Moto*, his eyes fixed on the vision above him. The angel was young and her face was beautiful. Her eyes brightened when she smiled at him. In that moment Aachim realized there were now hundreds of angels filling the sky. Softly at first, but growing louder, their voices began to sing out "Glory to God." The chorus filled the sky and poured over the hills like soft rain.

The angel spoke to Aachim, saying "You have nothing to fear. I come to proclaim good news to you! I am bringing you tidings of great joy to be shared by the whole people. This day in David's City a savior has been born to you, the Messiah, and Lord. Let this be a sign to you: in a manger you will find an infant wrapped in swaddling clothes."

In the light from the skies Aachim could see all the way down the hills toward Beth Lehem where the tent of his family was pitched. Leaving the sheep behind he ran, almost stumbling, down to his tent. By the time he reached the tent the angels had dissolved back into the starry night sky. Aachim's mother and father were already up, standing in front of the tent looking up at the stars. One star burned as bright as the moon and together the little family walked in its direction.

A crowd of shepherds had already gathered at the entrance to the animal manger behind Beth Lehem's inn. Aachim and his parents worked their way to the front of the crowd to see. Just as the angel had said, there was a woman holding a newborn baby. Their faces were golden in the flickering torch light. Aachim heard one of the shepherds share what he had learned. "They are Joseph and Mary from Nazareth. The child's name is Jesus."

They all stood staring at the scene. It was just as the angel had said. Aachim wondered what the angel's strange words meant when she said this child was to be a savior, a messiah?

Aachim felt his mother's hands gently rest upon his shoulders. He looked up into her brimming eyes and saw the forming tears. A warm breeze caressed them as they stood helplessly in awe and wonder.

✝

Each Christmas the world stands helplessly in awe and wonder among the shepherds who came to the manger on that first night. To wonder at the ways of God who chooses to be born unto us as a little baby. To marvel that God loves us enough to live and walk among us—a God who would die for us.

In this child is the great gift of eternal life. What more could we ask? It truly is the "Happiest night of the world!"

The Feast of the Holy Family
Luke 2: 22-40

The Knowing

It was the Jewish month of Abib, and in keeping with the tradition, the family of Jesus set out for Jerusalem where in the great temple, Jesus, as first-born son, would be consecrated and dedicated to God.

Joseph held the cage containing the two doves and smiled down at Mary, holding their son in her arms.

"I wish that we could give a year-old lamb as the offering," Mary said, shifting little Jesus to her other arm. She adjusted her shawl to shield his eyes from the sun. Looking to Joseph for an answer, Mary noticed a weariness in his face. They had been walking steadily since early morning.

"Because we have no flocks of our own," Joseph explained, "these doves are acceptable. One will be for adoration and the other for a sin offering."

Mary smiled silently as she thought about tomorrow. Ahead was the immense city and the lofty temple rising up on the mount. Joseph noticed Mary looking, wide-eyed, up at the fortress walls and the towers beyond. Jerusalem was exciting— the Great Temple, the merchants and markets, soldiers and strange people from foreign lands. Tonight Joseph and Mary and Jesus would sleep within its walls.

At the temple the next morning the Saducee priest Simeon eyed the trio coming toward him. He felt tired, wondering why he had risen so early and come to the temple this day. Simeon also noted that they only had caged doves for the offerings.

"Good morning Rabbi," Joseph said. "We want to dedicate our firstborn." Mary drew back her shawl so that Simeon could see the child.

Simeon looked down on the little face and a rush of realization swept over him. This was the special child, the one foretold. This was the Anointed of the Lord, the Messiah!

Simeon remembered his years of waiting. He remembered his times of doubt. He remembered the clear promise of the Spirit, now fulfilled before him.

The old man reached out to claim the child. Mary placed little Jesus in Simeon's arms and the old Rabbi's eyes brimmed with tears as he gently embraced his God.

✝

We, like Simeon, have heard the promise and we also wait for the coming of the Lord in our lives. The wonder-child waits too. Waiting for us to keep our appointment in that special time and place when we come to "the knowing."

The Epiphany of the Lord
Matthew 2: 1-12

The Epiphany of the Lord

Even before darkness young Aachim could see the new star burning through the day sky. Standing with the flock, he looked down the long slope that led to the empty Jerusalem Road. Looking in the uphill direction, the buildings of Beth Lehem were washed gold in the setting sunlight.

Aachim slowly followed the sheep as they grazed the rivers of grass flowing in the soft evening breeze. He gazed further up the hillside and decided not to go higher. It would be safer to stay near the town. Beside, Ruth's house was in Aachim's view and it would help him to pass the time by imagining her inside.

When darkness came Aachim began to circle the perimeter of the flock, watching his steps by the bright starlight overhead. As he went along he could almost make out his shadow. The hills seemed to be dusted with a pale white mist from the stars glittering above. He looked up at the star and was amazed by it's brightness.

In the murky distance down the Jerusalem Road Aachim saw that a caravan was heading his way. Searching his immediate area, Aachim saw movement across the field outside the stable behind Beth Lehem's travelers' inn. Two people were going into the shelter.

Aachim settled down to watch for awhile, glad that there were these diversions to help pass the night. Slowly the caravan continued up the road toward Bethlehem. The young shepherd reclined on his elbow and closed his eyes. He decided to rest for a moment, but reminded himself to keep his ears on alert. He fell asleep and dreamed of a night ablaze with stars and the sounds of people singing

A bleating lamb awoke him and Aachim blinked his eyes at the sight of three stately riders sitting tall atop their camels. They passed directly in front of him and headed toward the traveler's inn. Aachim watched in amazement as they dismounted and led their camels toward the stable where he had seen the other two earlier. The sheep seemed okay for the moment and Aachim hurried across the field to get a better look.

The three strange men had dropped to their knees at the entrance to the stable. Inside the dim flickers from the oil lamp revealed three more people

looking out at the foreigners. There was a man and his wife who was holding a newborn infant in her arms.

Aachim glanced back to make sure the flock was not moving. Their white backs were where he'd left them.

In turn each of the men returned to their camel and brought boxes from their packs which they gave to the family inside.

Hurrying back to the flock Aachim wondered about this strange event. He circled the flock, rounding up a few stragglers. He sat down and watched. The camels were still there, so the strangers were probably spending the night.

Aachim drifted on his thoughts, dozing off to sleep, then waking with a start and dozing again.

When he opened his eyes it was bright morning. He scrambled to his feet and surveyed the flock. All was well. Across the slope the camels were gone. He hurried down to the stable and looked inside. It was empty too. Aachim began to ask himself if all he'd seen had been a dream. Then he noticed a sweetness in the air. It was like perfume. At his feet were a few small jewel drops of shiny brown resin spilled on the smooth dirt floor. He picked up a resin pebble and held its rich aroma of frankincense to his nose.

✝

What the shepherd boy witnessed that night was a Mystery confirmed only by a few spilled pebbles of aromatic gum. In a few decades the same shepherd would be in Jerusalem for the Passover and would see the Mystery again.

Aachim's encounters are no more than our own. Each of us has been gifted with a few pebbles of recognition that confirm his presence in our lives. These confirmations lead us to our own epiphany of the Lord.

The Baptism of the Lord
Mark 1: 7-11

The Baptism
of the Lord

John the Baptist put his right hand on the back of Jesus' neck and gripped Jesus' arm with his other hand.

"Just lean back with me. I will guide you," John said as he eased Jesus backwards into the waist-deep water.

Jesus gasped as the cold water claimed him, flooding the warmth of his back and gushing up around his shoulders. As his head went underwater, Jesus held his breath and scrunched his eyes tightly shut. He could feel the current flowing past him. Floating just below the surface in the watery silence, Jesus felt peace come over him.

John held Jesus firmly, pushing him down into the Jordan. Through the rippling water, Jesus' face was framed with the dark crown of his swirling hair. John saw Jesus' tranquil expression, like that of a sleeping child. He wasn't struggling for air like most of the people John baptized.

The words of Isaiah and Ezekiel flowed into Jesus' mind; words about God's spirit being poured out like water, cleansing and empowering. John the Baptist was preaching that the baptism and repentance required of non-Jews now was necessary for everyone, even the Jews themselves. And John was truly a prophet. And Jesus had come to fulfill the prophecy.

Jesus' eyes burst open underwater, startling John. His eyes remained fixed on something in the sky as he stood up in the water. John backed away to behold Jesus, water streaming down his uplifted face.

Jesus saw the sky split open and fill with warmth and light. The shimmering light began to take a shape, forming itself into a white blur that suddenly resolved into a beautiful dove. Its wings opened and it began to descend toward Jesus, sending light rays shining down before it.

Jesus was overwhelmed with the presence of God filling the dove and overflowing into a Spirit which charged the air with electricity and then the scent of flowers.

A great voice spoke words that thundered across the skies and up the mountainsides, and out across the desert waste, and into every part of Jesus mind. They were words seemingly as immense as centuries of time—words encompassing all languages, words becoming all the sounds of the universe. All of this distilled itself into a tiny whisper which only Jesus could hear: "You are my beloved Son. On you my favor rests."

✝

In celebrating the Baptism of Jesus this Sunday, we also celebrate our own baptism—our rising up from the water to receive new life. We celebrate that we became Children of God. We celebrate our Confirmation when we received the Holy Spirit. We celebrate the gift of Communion as we share in the banquet of Christ's sacrifice. We celebrate our life, living as Christians so that in our dying we receive Eternal Life.

The
Lenten
Season

First Sunday of Lent
Mark 1: 12-15

The time
of fulfillment...

The weeks he'd spent alone in the desert had been hard on Jesus. He was lean from his fasting, almost gaunt. The sockets of his eyes were deepened with hunger. At age 30 the last of his youthfulness had been replaced with the hardened lines of manhood. There was a grim determination about him. Jesus had come face to face with the awesome reality of who he was and what he was becoming.

Coming to the banks of the Jordan again, Jesus hesitated a moment, remembering that day when John had immersed him and the voice had spoken. This day there were no crowds at the river. Only Jesus, only the wind. He picked his way down the riverbank and waded back into the waters where he had been baptized by John. The coldness washed the sand away and he drank deeply. Overhead the hot sun filled the sky and smiled down on Jesus, languishing in the river.

His moment of refreshment was soon ended, bad news was waiting. Entering the first village, Jesus asked where he could find John the Baptist.

"You haven't heard?" the old shopkeeper asked.

Jesus shook his head, "No."

The shopkeeper's eyes widened and he inclined his head toward Jesus, saying in a low voice, "John has been arrested. They've taken him to the prison."

Like startled birds rushing to flight, Jesus felt anxiety course through his body as he imagined himself being arrested. He closed his eyes, picturing John in chains somewhere. A moment later he opened his eyes to see the old shopkeeper, still waiting for more reaction from Jesus. "Are you one of John's disciples?" he asked.

"He baptized me," Jesus said flatly.

With John gone, Jesus decided to head north, back to Galilee. He would bring the news to Simon Peter and his brother Andrew and the others who had

known John. His time of fulfillment was at hand. He would now fully proclaim God's good news!

✝

Our lives are frequented by "desert experiences" that are difficult; times when it can't possibly get any worse, but it does. These times are the inevitable valleys through which we all must pass. These are the dark nights that seem never to end. There is only one hope for us in these times and places—Jesus, who is always there. He is as close as our prayer, as present as our thoughts allow him. Jesus will see us through to the dawn of a new day. Our faith is our strength.

Second Sunday in Lent
Mark 9: 2-10

Overcome with awe

Jesus had moved ahead of Peter, James and John and was standing under a field of light. It was as if a huge circle had been cut in the roof of the sky, and through it a powerful white light was pouring down onto the mountain top. Excess light seemed to hit the ground and splash like molten lava around where Jesus stood with his face uplifted to the heavens.

Peter, James and John huddled in the darkness outside the circle of light. They were overcome with awe.

The light continued to pour down in a waterfall of whiteness. In the midst of this, Jesus clothes became even whiter. The light was so dazzling the disciples had to sheild their squinting eyes.

Without warning two men appeared, standing in conversation with Jesus. The flickering forms of Moses and Elijah, the great prophets of the past, seemed now to be giving their authority to the new prophet, Jesus.

Afterwards the Disciples would make the connection between Moses and God meeting atop Mount Sinai and this meeting on the mountain top where Jesus had been awash in a celestial light.

Later, as they were coming down the mountain with Jesus, the night was full of the Disciples' amazed voices.

"I still can't believe it," Peter protested.

"There was a cloud that covered them. I couldn't see them inside of it," Andrew stammered.

"But you heard the voice, it was God's voice, wasn't it?" John declared and asked in the same sentence.

Jesus patiently let them try and piece it all together. Then, as they were nearing the foothills that would lead them home, he said to them. "Friends, I ask you not to tell anyone what you have seen and heard until the Son of Man has risen from the dead."

For a moment the four men walked on in silence. They had understood all but the last part of Jesus' request.

"Master," Peter asked, "are you saying you will rise from the dead?"

Jesus did not reply, but when his eyes met Peter's the answer was given. No one spoke again until they reached home.

☦

When Jesus was transfigured on the mountain top he allowed Andrew, John, Peter and you and I the privilege to see God's favor poured out upon the earth. This favor is still visible in the beauties of the world around us and the blessed people in our lives. During Lent, it we take a close look at ourselves we may also see God's glory and favor there as well. When we follow Jesus more closely the Light seems to intensify

Third Sunday of Lent
John 2: 13-45

The whip
of cords...

Jesus slashed downward with the whip he had made from thick cords. The whip cracked hard across a table, overturning it and spilling everything out onto the floor. Jesus was breathing hard as he shouted: "Stop turning my Father's house into a marketplace!" He was clutching the whip so tightly he had to remind himself to relax his grip.

The once business-like order of the temple courtyard was now a scene of chaos. Escaping doves fluttered overhead. Untethered oxen were wandering through the jumble of tables and boxes. Jesus surveyed the aftermath of his work.

The cursing moneychangers were still scrambling to find all the coins that were spilled when Jesus overturned their tables. One of them was on his hands and knees, groveling for his coins. He angrily looked up at Jesus and spat at him.

Other vendors were rolling up their wares and retreating. A crowd of onlookers had quickly gathered, forming a circle which enclosed the temple courtyard. One man from the crowd, hoping to see a fight, shouted at Jesus: "Who do you think you are with your whip and your big mouth?"

Another voice added: "He must be crazy."

"Get the Rabbi," another urged.

Jesus knew their hearts and lamented. The people had little time for God. They had little concern for their temple which had been reduced to a public market. They had even less interest in Jesus' message. There was a pall of hopelessness now draped about the scene. They would all be back again in the morning.

"What sign can you show us authorizing you to do these things," someone asked.

Jesus turned to him and answered. "Destroy this temple," he began, placing his hands on his own chest to indicate he was talking about the temple of his body, "and I will raise it up in three days."

A ripple of laughter went through the crowd. One of them, thinking Jesus was talking about the temple building, said "This temple took 46 years to build and you're going to raise it up in three days?"

Jesus smiled back and nodded.

The Disciples who were there would one day recall the great resurrection prophecy given that day by Jesus.

✝

Lent charges into our lives once a year, overturning our tables. Lent challenges us to think about our interests, our passions and our transgressions. Lent reminds us that there are troubled "temple precincts" in our own lives. Lent asks us to examine the way we live and the integrity of our relationship with God. During Lent we may uncover obstacles which keep us from living our faith. Jesus asks us "What's this doing in your life? Get it out, it's blocking your path to me." Then Jesus will hand us his whip of cords, allowing us to use it to drive the obstacles away.

Fourth Sunday of Lent
John 3: 14-21

The Diary
of Nicodemus

The scratches of black ink flowed onto the first page of the scroll as Nicodemus began to record what Jesus had told him. The letters danced in the flickering light from the oil lamp on his desk. He had to put a weight on the top end of the scroll to hold it flat until the ink was dry. The words had been freshly been spoken to Nicodemus earlier that night when he had gone to meet Jesus.

Nicodemus looked out his window at the rooftops of Jerusalem. The city was asleep under its blanket of starlight. The deserted streets flowed like black rivers meandering between the buildings.

He began to write again, recalling the words Jesus had spoken: "God so loved the world that he gave his only Son..." Nicodemus paused as he tried to understand that Jesus was that son. He dipped his pen into the ink and continued "...that whoever believes in him may not die but have everlasting life."

Nicodemus wondered if he would really have everlasting life. He certainly believed in Jesus enough to visit him, even if those cautious night visits were made under cover of darkness, and in secret. As a high-ranking Pharisee, Nicodemus had to be very careful about the people he was seen with. Because of Jesus' preaching and growing popularity he was considered dangerous. Yet, Nicodemus was powerfully drawn to him.

As Nicodemus wrote these next words onto the scroll, he wondered if Jesus was challenging him to make his next visit in broad daylight. He wrote: "Everyone who practices evil hates the light; he does not come near it for fear his deeds will be exposed." Nicodemus knew Jesus was right as he concluded his notes: "But he who acts in truth comes into the light, to make clear that his deeds are done in God."

One day Nicodemus would come into the light when he defended Jesus before the other chief priests. On another day the Light would shine most brightly on Nicodemus as he purchased costly myrrh and aloes and helped Joseph of Arimathea wrap Jesus' body and lay him in the tomb.

✝

    We come into the light with Nicodemus when we publicly profess our faith. Not by bragging, but by living as active Christians. We remain in the dark when we do not truly believe that God so loved the world that he gave us his beloved Son so that he could then give us eternal life? When we are ready to proclaim that message—then we have stepped into the public light and God's light shines through us for all the world to see.

Fifth Sunday of Lent
John 12: 20-33

Glorify thy name!

Jerusalem was teeming with people. Pilgrims from all parts of the Mediterranean world had come to celebrate the feast of the Passover. Among them were two adventurous God-seekers who had journeyed all the way from Greece. These Greeks were not Jews and were among the first of the Gentiles to seek the God proclaimed through Jesus. The Greeks' fascination with Jesus had become intense when they learned that Jesus had raised a man called Lazarus from the dead.

The crowds moved slowly among the sprawl of stalls and stands where the sellers camped at the Damascus Gate. The two Greeks made their way inside the walls of the city searching for the Temple courtyard. They wandered through the winding streets, passing shops which wafted their sharp aromas of leather, spice, and fruits.

When they reached the Temple, the Greeks searched among the crowd for Jesus. Asking around, they said: "Have you seen the one, they say, who raised a man from the dead over in Bethany?"

"You mean Jesus?" one of the Jews confirmed.

"Yes, we'd like to meet him," the Greek replied.

"He's over there with his friends," the Jew smiled, pointing across the courtyard to a large group of young men who were laughing and talking together. The Greeks crossed over to the outside edge the group. Philip, who himself was just arriving, looked over at the two foreigners. One of the Greeks caught Philip's eye. "Sir, we wish to see Jesus."

"You're Greeks?" Philip asked.

"Yes, we've come a long way to find him."

"He is the one standing at the top of the steps. Wait here, I'll see what I can do," Philip said. He began working his way through the crowd toward Jesus. He found Andrew at the bottom of the Temple steps and told him about the two Greeks. Together, they went up the steps and told Jesus. He nodded and his eyes scanned the crowd. When Jesus saw the two Greeks standing at the outer edge of the crowd, he began to preach. He was looking directly at them as he proclaimed: "The hour has come..."

That day Jesus told how a grain of wheat must die to bear its fruit. He spoke of how believers must die to receive eternal life. He reassured his followers that his Father would honor them. He revealed his human fear of accepting his Father's will, but his divine resolve to accept his own imminent death.

Then, shouting to the sky, Jesus prayed: "Father, glorify thy name!"

Like a great roll of thunder, a voice came booming back from the heavens: "I have glorified it and I will glorify it again."

The two Greeks stood transfixed, overwhelmed in silent rapture. They had not only found Jesus, but in the thunder they had heard the very voice of God!

✝

Like the Greek adventurers, each day of our lives we must journey to our own "Jerusalem." There we are challenged to find Jesus in our midst. We might encounter "Philips and Andrews" who will help us to discover him. If we seek, we shall find. And when we find him, when we recognize him, if we wait in love and silence, we, too, will be privileged to hear the thunderous voice of God speaking deep within our own hearts.

Passion Sunday
Mark 14: 1 – 15: 47

The Anointing...

The warm afternoon air began to cool as the shadows on the walls of Simon's house softened in the golden light of approaching sunset. Jesus and the Disciples were listening to Simon re-tell the story of the ghastly years when he was unclean with leprosy. Simon's glowing complexion was bronzed in the golden light as he told how Jesus' miraculous healing had restored his health. Simon continued, describing how he had also reclaimed his former wealth. His grateful glances honored Jesus.

Staying at Simon's home in Bethany had been a great blessing for Jesus and the Disciples. Jerusalem was a madhouse. The streets were jammed with thousands of pilgrims who poured through its gates to celebrate the feasts of the Passover and the Unleavened Bread. As Simon's honored guests, Jesus and his friends reclined at the table which soon would be filled with good things to eat. Jesus eased himself back onto the cushions and studied the deepening colors of the western sky.

One of Simon's servants interrupted to announce that a woman had come with perfume for Jesus.

"Bring her to us," Simon ordered, waving for her to enter.

When the servant brought the woman to the doorway of the room, she stood there, searching for Jesus among the fourteen faces who looked up at her. She was cradling a white alabaster jar with both of her hands. Recognizing Jesus she moved boldly toward him. "May I anoint you, Lord?" she asked.

Jesus opened his hands to her in assent. She knelt by him and broke the top seal of the jar. The scent of the fine oil floated out to the Disciples who silently watched as she smoothed the oil onto Jesus' face and forehead.

"This is like the anointing of Jehu," one of the Disciples said, recalling the ancient Prophet Elisha's directions for anointing Jehosaphat's son as king of Israel.

As the woman continued to anoint Jesus feet and the rest of his body, Judas grumbled, "What is the point of this extravagant waste of perfume?" The entire jar was now used on Jesus. "It could have been sold for a year's wages and given to the poor!"

"Why do you criticize her?" Jesus asked. "She has done me a kindness. The poor you will always have with you and you can be generous to them whenever you wish. You will not always have me."

None of the Disciples could look him in the eye when Jesus explained that the woman had just anointed his body for burial.

The silent men all stared at their hands, except for Judas who had risen to his feet and was edging toward the door.

✝

The story of the kingly anointing at Bethany prepares us for Jesus' kingly entry into Jerusalem amid the palms. The anointing as a preparation for burial prepares us for the awful reality that Jesus will be betrayed. These contrasts reveal the good and evil which is a part of human life. This calls us to deep reflection on our place in the Passion story. Are we the woman who brought the precious oils? Are we one of the disciples, even Judas, or perhaps part of the condemning crowd?

Easter Season through the Sundays of the Lord

Easter Sunday
John 20: 1-9

Discovery!

The sun burst through the horizon and splashed golden light against the eastern walls of Jerusalem's buildings. The dawn had yet to find its way into the deserted streets that meandered between the buildings. The silent corridors were still gloomy alleys where the last of the cold night could hide from the sun.

Mary Magdalen shook Peter's shoulder, and shouted in the dark room. "Jesus' body is not in the tomb!"

Startled from his sleep, Peter forced one angry eye open and glared up at Mary, kneeling at his side. "What?" he demanded.

"The Lord has been taken from the tomb! We don't know where they have put him," Mary repeated.

By then John was awake, propping himself up on an elbow. Peter looked at Mary's tear streaked face and pondered what she had said. After a long moment he pulled on his robe and sandals.

"Gone?" he asked her.

Mary nodded.

John hurried into his clothes and nearly collided with Peter as they both rushed for the door.

The silence of the streets was broken with the noise of Peter and John running to the garden where the tomb had been dug.

They were running as fast as they could through the winding streets. Peter started to fall behind.

Peter shouted ahead to John, "Wait up!" John didn't look back. Fueled by his exasperation, Peter struggled furiously to keep going. Pain burned in the muscles of his legs and a painful knot was beginning to form in his chest.

As he continued to run, Peter wondered what happened. Who would steal the body of Jesus? It might have been soldiers or even thieves. Perhaps Mary and the other women had simply gone to the wrong tomb.

John was waiting at the entrance to Jesus' tomb when Peter limped the last few steps. Gasping with exhaustion, he stared at the huge stone which had been rolled away. Peter did not hesitate. He stepped past John and crouched inside the tomb. The body wrappings were heaped in a pile on the ground. On

the ledge, folded neatly, was the blood-stained cloth that had covered Jesus' face.

John came in and knelt on one knee next to Peter. He put his hand on Peter's back to keep his balance. The two men were so filled with wonder they could not speak. Slowly they began to accept the reality of the Resurrection that had taken place.

✝

Like Mary Magdalen and the other women we discover the reality of this most important moment of all time. Like Peter and John, we can kneel in the empty tomb and finally come to know that Jesus is Risen. Like every Christian through the centuries we will eventually know that by His Resurrection, Jesus beckons us also to rise with him. May all of these truths flow to us this Easter and fill us with God's joy and love.

Second Sunday of Easter
John 20: 19-31

'I send you!'

Those who saw him stumbling down the stairs must have thought Peter was drunk. When he reached the street he began walking in a daze. Jesus had just appeared for the second time. The doors had been locked, the windows closed. Yet, Jesus was suddenly in their midst. Thomas had even stuck his fingers into the wounds from the cross and the sword. Like God breathing life into Adam, Jesus had breathed on them. Peter's mind was drenched with the miracle it could not contain. Peter staggered through the streets as the downpour of thoughts pelted him like raindrops.

The Feast of the Unleavened Bread was now over and Peter shouldered his way through the crowds of pilgrims who were exiting the city. People had flocked into Jerusalem to be present for these high holy days. They had come from all the cities of Judah and Idumea, Edom, Decapolis and Galilee. Now, loaded with purchases, they were hurrying home. Seeing them about him, Peter began to think about his own return to Galilee. He wondered how the boat was doing with no one to tend it.

He hadn't noticed, but his brother Andrew was walking at his side. Andrew pulled Peter to a stop. Their eyes met in silent exchange of the experience they had just shared. "Where are you going?" Andrew asked, since Peter had seemed to be wandering. Peter rubbed his hands together and looked around him for fear of the authorities that might be looking for the rest of Jesus' followers.

"I don't know. I was thinking about the boat. I'm trying to decide what to do now. He must want us to go back to Galilee. Last week Mary told us that, remember?"

Andrew nodded. "It's dangerous to stay here in Jerusalem.

In the midst of Andrew's sentence, Jesus' freshly spoken words suddenly returned to Peter: "He said send. We should go now. Andrew, go tell the rest. Jesus said 'I send you,' remember?"

The downpour of thoughts continued to deluge Peter. To be "sent" also meant he was starting a solemn mission. All that Jesus had taught and preached had to somehow continue. A strange peace soothed Peter and without words,

he knew that he was being filled with courage, grace and power.

The disciples left Jerusalem separately, mingling in with the crowds of departing Pilgrims. As Peter passed unnoticed under the Damascus gate he felt a soar of excitement course through him. Following the north road he began to smile to himself. He knew he was no longer alone. God was with him, Jesus was at his side, and the Holy Spirit had completely filled his heart.

☦

In each of our lives Jesus appears. Just as he came to the Disciples in the secret locked room, he comes in the secret of our locked heart. There, where no one else may go, he finds us and fills us with peace and says "As the father has sent me, so I send you." And with those words he commissions us to love one another, to forgive one another, and to hold one another accountable. Like Peter, we are filled with the courage to take a stand and to stand up for what is right and just. It is then that we truly become Christians, followers of the Risen Lord Jesus Christ.

Third Sunday of Easter
Luke 24: 35-48

The Message

Peter was hanging upside down on a cross. The blood pounded and pulsed in his head and searing pain raced everywhere through his body. He struggled for dignity, but Peter's defiant eyes were bulging in and out of focus.

The two Roman centurions watching him die were bored. They stalked about, jabbing the butts of their spears against the rocky ground. The chinking sound brought Peter back to consciousness. The guards seemed to be upside down, dangling from the earth. Then Peter remembered, he was upside down. The guards' voices grew fainter as Peter's mind rushed him away to remember that miraculous day near Bethany when the Risen Jesus had walked and talked with them. At first the eleven disciples didn't notice there was a twelfth man in their midst. Suddenly they realized it was Jesus!

Peter remembered trying to reach out and touch the Master, but his body wouldn't respond. He was so filled with joy he couldn't move. He had just listened as Jesus told them again to preach in his name to all the nations.

The warm memory exploded in new pain. Gasping, Peter knew that he had really tried to follow Jesus' instruction to preach to the nations. He preached, even unto his end here in distant Rome.

Peter remembered how he had been asked to preach that people should be sorry for their sins. Peter could never forget the sound of the rooster crowing that day they had seized Jesus. He still wanted to cry out "I'm sorry," but he had no way. Being crucified upside down was not enough penance. Peter realized his own crucifixion seemed more of a privilege than a penance.

Just beyond Rome's green hills, in the distance, Peter saw a white-robed man rushing toward him. He knew the familiar smile. Peter was smiling too as he struggled to break free from his cross and run to the welcoming arms of the Master.

The next day, when the centurions returned to untie Peter's body from the cross, one of them noticed a curious thing. He bent over and cocked his head toward the ground to better look at Peter's lifeless face.

"Hey, look," the centurion exclaimed. "This guy is smiling."

✝

The Gospel message we receive today leaves all of us with the same directions from our Risen Jesus. He tells us penance for the remission of sins must be preached to all nations. He told the disciples and he tells us: "You are witnesses of this." The command to preach to all nations is overwhelming. Jesus told the disciples to begin at Jerusalem. Jesus tells us to begin where we are in our own town, on our own street, in our own house and in our very own heart. After that heaven only knows.

Fourth Sunday of Easter
John 10: 11-18

The Good Shepherd

Jesus stared into the fire and remembered.

It had been an extraordinary day! It had begun down by the little harbor at Capernaum. He and the disciples had breakfasted on the rock wall by the shore of the lake while Peter checked the mooring lines on the boat. But soon, the crowds began to form.

During the slow and easy morning, they followed the south road out from Capernaum. Jesus remembered how he and the disciples were followed by a growing throng as they made their way up the slopes. On the hill crest, beneath the grove, everyone stopped to enjoy the magnificent view of the entire lake. It sprawled like a bright blue blanket on the golden valley. A flowing breeze rustled through the tall stand of trees. It was a good place to spend the day. After everyone had eaten and rested, Jesus rose, like a shepherd from his resting flock. Jesus remembered how his words had poured out powerfully to the listeners sitting before him in the Spring grass.

By mid-afternoon the people began to disperse, heading back to their homes. When they were gone, Jesus and the disciples climbed deeper into the hill country. The warm night had descended on them and was now filled with the scent of roasting lamb, wafting from the crackling fire. Jesus watched the flames and felt peace soothe him.

From the corner of his eye, Jesus saw some movement on the hill below. A silent flock was passing north. The shepherd, like the mast of a ship, stood tall in the midst of his flock. They moved together in unison. The sheep and the shepherd were like one being, blended in the dusky night.

Jesus turned to his disciples. The firelight lit his face in dancing amber strokes.

"I am the good shepherd," he began.

"The good shepherd lays down his life for his sheep." The disciples looked at him, wondering, not yet ready to realize his dark prophecy.

✝

The shepherd always watches over his flock. The Good Shepherd Jesus watches over us. We are his flock today. He has his eye on each person. If we get into trouble or wander too far, he is there to help us and lead us home.

He stokes the mighty furnace of the sun to warm us through the day. He turns down the covers of the night and leaves the starlight on to watch over our sleep. What then is fear? How is it that we worry? We are safe in his keeping. He is our Good Shepherd.

Fifth Sunday of Easter
John 15: 1-8

The Vineyard

James popped a grape in his mouth and savored its tartness.
"Not quite ripe," he said to Jesus.

The grapevine twisted along the trellis like a thick rope. Jesus studied it,
then he plunged his hands into the shade of the leaves. His fingers traced the

48

branches and canes down to their source and he grasped the strong vine. Looking up at the disciples, he shook the vine and declared: "I am the true vine."

The disciples weren't sure if this was the beginning of a lesson, or if Jesus was merely making a comment. They waited.

As if remembering something, Jesus continued to speak without looking up at them.

"My Father is the vine grower."

Jesus snapped off a brown leaf and let it fall to the ground.

"Every barren branch, he prunes away." Jesus found a fat branch, heavy with grapes, and stripped away some small growth. "But the fruitful ones he trims clean to increase their yield."

Philip selected a grape for himself and made a sour face, spitting the pulp away. He laughed at James who was grinning at him for not heeding his warning that the grapes were too tart.

When Philip noticed that Jesus was also looking at him, he thought there might be a question, so he began to review what Jesus had just said. The long vine had many branches. The branches all depend on the vine to bring the moisture and nourishment from the ground. Jesus said he was that vine. Philip smiled in understanding.

"Because we follow you, would you say we are your branches?" Philip asked.

Jesus nodded his head. Then he put his arms around the shoulders of the disciples closest to him. Hugging them, he said: "My Father has been glorified in your bearing much fruit and becoming my disciples."

This Gospel reading tells us of our complete dependence on Jesus, the vine. The reading lets us know that for all of our strength, wisdom and ability, we are only the branches. The reading also tells us that we are expected to bear fruit. In one brilliant image, Jesus tells us who he is, who we are and what we are expected to do. He even tells us that if we do not bear fruit, his Father, the gardener, will prune away every barren branch.

Sixth Sunday of Easter
John 15: 9-17

Love one another!

The warm red wine burned in his throat, but the Disciple John swallowed anyway. The other disciples were chewing their bread and sipping the harsh wine as they reclined around the table with Jesus.

John was uncomfortable with what Jesus had been saying. Everything the Teacher had spoken seemed like final instructions. It was as if Jesus was about to leave them. John did not want to see any changes. He didn't want Jesus to leave.

Jesus was almost smiling as he leaned back on his elbow, savoring the company and the silence. He took his time, thinking of what he was going to say next.

John was still reflecting on what Jesus had just told them about keeping commandments—how Jesus was keeping his father's commandments and how, if John was to abide in Jesus' love, he would have to keep the commandments of Jesus. And just when John was trying to remember what the commandments were, Jesus sat upright and rose to his feet.

John watched Jesus take his time, making eye-contact with each of the disciples. Whatever he was going to say now, John thought, it will be something very important.

"This is my commandment," Jesus said, "that you love one another as I have loved you."

John felt the enormity of what this meant. He would have to love others as much as he loved Jesus—and he loved Jesus a lot! It would be an almost impossible commandment to follow. Even among the disciples it was difficult to love one another. They had grown close to each other over these years together, but even still there were times when there was no love between them.

Jesus continued speaking: "There is no greater love than this: to lay down one's life for one's friends. You are my friends if you do what I command you. I no longer speak of you as slaves, for a slave does not know what his master is about. Instead, I call you friends, since I made known to you all that I heard from my Father. It was not you who chose me, it was I who chose you to go forth and bear fruit. Your fruit must endure, so that all you ask the father in my name he will give you."

Jesus sat back down, took a final sip of the wine, and said again: "The command I give you is this, that you love one another."

Jesus speaks with such brilliance! What other command could be so all-encompassing as this? If we truly love one another then every other commandment must be obeyed. If we truly love one another there can be none of the evils that live in our midst: no hunger, no homelessness, no cruelty and no violence. Loving one another conquers everything.

The Ascension of the Lord
Mark 16: 15-20

Proclaim the Good News

The warm south wind was blowing stronger on the mountain top. It billowed the robes of Jesus as he stood at the highest point of the Mount of Olives. Jesus' face was uplifted now and a lightness seemed to be shining from it.

Peter, standing with the rest of the eleven disciples, was reminded of the night when Jesus was transfigured on another mountaintop in Galilee. The group of mystified disciples formed a protective circle around Jesus as he began to rise and dissolve before them. And then, suddenly he was gone. Only the wind remained.

It took a long time for the disciples to realize what they had just experienced. So many images raced in their minds: Jesus dragging his heavy cross; the brutal nailing and raising of the cross; the anguish and weeping and his death. They remembered the darkening of the heavens, Jesus' burial, the stone, the discovery by the women and the astonishing revelation that he had risen from the dead. They held the vision of his appearances at Emmaus, in the room at Jerusalem, on the shore in Galilee and now, here, again.

Peter became the new center of the circle of disciples. He was wondering what to do when he looked west toward Jerusalem. From across the Kidron Valley Peter could see the entire city. From where they stood Jerusalem didn't look so formidable. The final instructions of Jesus had been "Go into the whole world and proclaim the good news to all creation." They would begin in Jerusalem.

With courage and strength building in his heart, Peter began to lead the disciples back down the Bethany Road toward the lofty fortress walls of Jerusalem.

As the group of disciples made their way down the winding mountain trail, the fullness of God's presence was poured into them. They received the power of faith. They remembered the last words of Jesus: "...use my name to expel demons...speak entirely new languages...handle serpents...drink deadly poison without harm...and the sick upon whom they lay their hands will recover."

Waves of rapturous joy swept through the returning band of disciples as the presence of Jesus continued to shower down upon them. They felt as if Jesus was walking at their side. His love and his life were being reborn in their hearts.

☦

Jesus' final instructions were to his eleven remaining disciples. If we count ourselves in that modern-day number, then Jesus speaks to us as well. He says "...if you believe you will be saved. If you refuse to believe you will be condemned." This belief gives us the power to go out and proclaim the good news to all creation.

Pentecost Sunday
Acts 2: 1-11, John 20: 19-23

The winds of Pentecost

The Roman Centurion standing atop the fortress wall watched the roadway leading north from Jerusalem. With the bountiful Spring harvest there had been a steady movement of traffic bearing grain into the city. Under a darkening sky, the Centurion noticed one man running toward Herod's Gate. As he struggled up the hill he was barely passing the slow moving caravans.

Peter had been jogging hard, but the final hill slowed him to a walk. He was late for the meeting with the disciples and friends of Jesus. A fresh gust of wind swirled up a cloud of dust as Peter walked briskly under the gate and into the city. Once inside, he followed the narrow street to the meeting house.

He was welcomed into the house and found it packed with people. Peter smiled greetings, put his arm around shoulders and gripped hands as he made his way toward the open breezeway that joined the inner garden patio with the main room of the house. Still breathing heavily from the running he headed to the inner garden for more air.

When Peter stepped into the open, the roaring sound began. It was a deep, moaning sound of powerful wind. Looking skyward, what hair Peter had began to fly wildly about his head. The warm wind poured over him like a fast flowing river of water. He felt a smile rising on his face as joy filled his heart. This wind had a "presence" in it and Peter knew it must be Jesus.

Everyone was now on their feet in alarm as the roaring wind swallowed up their shouts and cries of fear. The roar was terrifying. Those in the house struggled past each other to escape into the open garden and squint up at the dazzling sky. They saw long streamers of light begin to float down from the clouds, hanging like tentacles. Peter, grinning in fearless joy saw one of the streamers of light come spiraling down at him. With a snap, it struck Peter on his lips. It tingled, leaving a salty after-taste in his mouth.

"Pneuma!" Peter shouted in perfect Greek, startled both at what he said and that he also knew the word meant "spirit."

All that Jesus had said was being fulfilled. The Holy Spirit had been sent to them, just as Jesus promised.

✝

Today, the same Holy Spirit that was visited upon the first Christians, is now present in us. God has not abandoned us. We discover him in the Spirit, moving like a wind through our lives and through the world in which we live. If we can be silent for a moment we can discover that he is within us already. With the courage of faith we can move out of our safe places and into the raging wind where we can look up in confidence for the long streamers of light that can dance down from the skies and ignite our hearts with love and peace and joy.

The Most Holy Trinity
Mt. 28: 16-20

Make disciples
of all nations

The Risen Jesus had called the disciples to meet him on a mountain in Galilee. The disciples were on their way, hurrying up the steep path. Peter, balding and overweight, was remembering all the other mountains he had climbed with Jesus. Glancing back he saw his familiar Galilee below—a blue blanket of water smoothed flat among the surrounding foothills.

Peter had climbed a mountain to hear Jesus preach the beatitudes; he had climbed a mountain to be in the dazzling light when Jesus was transfigured; he had climbed the Mount of Olives when Jesus ascended into the skies. Now, here he was again, legs aching, heart pounding, gasping for air, climbing mountains for Jesus.

The figure at the top of the mountain was silhouetted in sunlight. It was hard to make out the details. Peter's eyes tried to focus. The other disciples were all well ahead of Peter. When he saw them dropping to their knees, Peter knew it was Jesus standing at the top.

Jesus appeared before them in sharp reality. Peter clutched his heaving chest and gratefully dropped to his knees. It was overwhelming—Jesus presence filled not only his eyes, but filled his heart. Exhaustion was instantly replaced with soaring joy.

For the disciples, the rapture of this intense oneness with Jesus erased the world below them. Time was suspended. The sounds of the world were muffled and only the clear words of Jesus could be heard.

Andrew felt as if the sky were not only above him but below him as well. The vision of Jesus seemed to lift him into a crystal clearness.

Jesus walked toward them and proclaimed: "Full authority has been given to me both in heaven and on earth; go, therefore, and make disciples of all the nations. Baptize them in the name of the Father and of the Son and of the Holy Spirit."

A revelation swept Peter's mind. God the Father sent his son Jesus who sends his Spirit. And Peter began to know that he was a servant to the Spirit.

Jesus continued. "Teach them to carry out everything I have command-ed you. And know that I am with you always, until the end of the world!"

The disciples had been fearful when Jesus commanded them to go to all nations baptizing and teaching. But the monumental task seemed simple now that Jesus had said he would be with them always. Peter smiled confidently. The whole world was waiting and he was excited to begin his ministry.

Jesus had filled him with his Spirit. Now anything would be possible.

☦

How well are we modern-day Christians doing with Jesus command-ment to go out and preach to all nations? How are we doing with just our-selves. Have we made ourselves disciples of Jesus? Have we lived up to our own baptism? Have we carried out everything Jesus has commanded? Do we know that Jesus is with us always, until the end of the world?

The Body and Blood of Christ
Mark: 14: 12-16, 22-26

This is my body...

Philip and Bartholomew were waiting by the rainwater cistern. They were the first to see him. He was a stocky little man who had just filled a large water jar. He wrapped both arms around the heavy jar and lifted. As he hurried down the street the round belly of the jar rolled against his own round belly causing occasional slops of water to leap free of the container and splash onto his servant's tunic.

The entire group of Disciples, led by Philip and Bartholomew, followed the man with the jar. As Jesus instructed them, they followed him to a large two-story house and watched him enter it. The Disciples then went to the front door.

Another servant answered, surprised at such a large group outside.

Peter spoke: "Tell your master that the Teacher asks where is my guest room where I may eat the Passover with my Disciples."

The owner was soon at the door and invited the group inside. He led them down a cool portico, flanked by gardens, past the main part of the house, they came to an outside stairway which ascended to a large room overlooking the gardens and the busy street outside the wall.

The owner smiled and with a sweep of his hand gestured toward two of his servants. "Everything you will need should be here for you. If there is more, these men will provide it."

The Disciples were amazed that everything Jesus had told them was now being fulfilled. With trembling hands they began to prepare what was to be their final supper with Jesus.

When Jesus appeared, all was ready. In each of their hearts a feeling of anxiety and sadness began to rise. John tried to contain his surging emotions and found himself near tears. Only Judas seemed unmoved. He had other things on his mind.

Jesus then took the bread and broke it. He held it up for all to see and solemnly declared: "This is my body..."

   Those words of Jesus have echoed through the Liturgy of the Eucharist for two millennia. They are the familiar words spoken by the celebrant at each Mass. They are words that summon us to the spiritual banquet which leads us into the depths of Jesus' love for us.

The Sundays of Ordinary Time

Second Sunday in Ordinary Time
John 1: 35:42

Come and See

Andrew felt a bolt of excitement race through his body when he heard John the Baptist say to him: "Look! There is the Lamb of God." Andrew looked up just in time to see Jesus turn a corner and disappear down one of the small streets of the town.

With the Baptist's other disciple, John, Andrew ran after Jesus to catch up with him. Surprised at their sudden departure, John the Baptist was left with an amused look on his face.

Jesus heard the foot-steps of the two disciples running up behind him and quickly turned to face them. Andrew and John slowed to a walk, holding back a little. Jesus saw they were keeping a respectful distance, meaning him no harm.

"What are you looking for?" Jesus asked.

"Rabbi, where are you staying?"

"Come and see." Jesus said.

The afternoon heat was sometimes scorching in the plain that lay across the Jordan on the lower slopes of lofty Jebel Yusha, highest mountain in Gilead. In the town of Bethany the air was motionless. The heat was unable to escape, trapped between the oven-like walls of the mountain ranges that straddled the Jordan valley.

As Jesus, Andrew and John moved slowly along the street, no-one wanted to break the heavy silence of the late afternoon. Conversation would have to wait until they found shade and refuge from the hot blanket of heat that smothered about them.

When they arrived at the place where Jesus was staying he made them welcome and they sat inside. Andrew and John loosened their clothing and began to realize how desperately thirsty they were. Jesus brought them water and they drank and began to talk.

For Andrew and John, the words Lamb of God meant both lamb and also servant of God. As Jesus spoke to them through the remainder of the afternoon and into the night it was clear to both that the words also meant Messiah. Andrew and John had indeed found the long-awaited Messiah—the Anointed One..

At first light the next morning, Andrew was off to find his brother, Simon, and tell him the good news. John went to find James.

Arriving back where Jesus stayed, Andrew and Simon stood silent. Jesus looked upon Simon for the first time. It was a moment of recognition, for this was the man who would one day lead the Church that Jesus would raise.

Eyes fixed on one another, Jesus declared: "You are Simon, son of John; your name shall be Peter."

✟

In each of our lives are many moments of recognition. We discover our bliss, our passion in life; our first love. Fortunately, we each discover Jesus in our own way, on our own "road to Emaus." We recognize him in the breaking of the bread.

One of Rudyard Kipling's poems speaks of friendship, saying that when we find worthy friends we should "bind them to our soul with hoops of steel." May your encounter with Christ bind you to him with hoops made of love— unbreakable hoops that will last for this lifetime and beyond.

3rd Sunday in Ordinary time
Mark 1: 14-20

'I will make you fishers of men!'

The sound of crunching gravel marked the cadence as Jesus marched steadily northward, toward the big grove of trees on the horizon. The giant trees marked the southern shore of the Sea of Galilee. With roots deep in the rich delta soil the trees drank from the saturating waters where the lake overflowed into the Jordan River.

Before sundown Jesus knew that he would be standing in the breeze, looking out on the broad expanse of the dark blue sea. He would spend the night under the trees. That night Jesus would try not to think about John's ghastly beheading. When Herod's men had taken John the Baptist off to prison, Jesus felt as if he were being taken too. Icy horror gripped Jesus when he later learned that the axeman had chopped off John's head. Like a sky filled with flocks of blackbirds, a foreboding anxiety descended on Jesus' mind. He faced a long night alone with his chattering thoughts. In the quiet of morning, at first light, Jesus would continue on up to Capernaum where he would seek his disciples.

With the first warming rays of the morning sun, Jesus felt happiness begin to fill him. This was the day! It was finally time to really begin to preach his message of repentance. He longed to see everyone changing from lives of sin to sanctity. He wanted people to believe the message of their salvation. Jesus was so eager to start that he began to jog along the path that led from the trees to the main road. Then it would be north to Tiberias and finally on to Capernaum.

It was evening when Capernaum came into view. Jesus was tired and anxious to find Peter and his brother Andrew. Perhaps there would be a tasty fish dinner and then a good night's sleep. He was hurrying along the shore road heading toward the fishing harbor when he saw them. They were fishing a short distance offshore. Peter had just made a powerful cast of his net. It flew out from the boat and floated beautifully down onto the surface of the water. Jesus felt a jolt of excitement rise in his throat as he called out to them, "Peter!

Andrew! Hello!"

Standing in the boat they looked up, squinting against the sunset to make out the figure silhouetted on the shore. When they recognized Jesus, Andrew bellowed happily across the water: "Hello, Jesus. We're catching lots of fish!"

Jesus shouted back, lifting his arm in an arc, motioning toward Capernaum. "Follow me and I will make you fishers of men!"

Peter and Andrew never even hauled in the net they had just cast. They let it sink. Hoisting sail they steered the boat toward the harbor on the last puffs of the gentle evening breeze.

✝

Jesus comes along the shores of our lives, calling out to us as he did to Andrew and Peter in their boat. He calls us by name, inviting us to "Repent and believe in the Gospel." From where we are in our busy schedules we may have to squint against the glare of the world's attractions to see Jesus silhouetted there. We may have to strain to identify him, but sooner or later we all will. The next step is the big question. Are we willing to let our nets sink where they're cast? Are we willing to let go and let God really happen in our lives?

4th Sunday in Ordinary Time
Mark 1: 21-28

'The Holy One of God...'

Jesus was reflecting deeply and did not look up at them. Yet, every eye in the synagogue at Capernaum was upon him. Jesus sat on his bench, hunched forward with his elbows on his knees, his hands slowly washing each other.

Jesus' commentaries on the readings were so brilliant that the congregation eagerly awaited his teaching. No one else dared to speak, completely deferring to him. In the golden hue of the oil lamps, their sepia faces were full of anticipation as the men waited for Jesus to begin.

Their peaceful mediation was shattered when a man came through the doorway of the synagogue and began shouting. He seemed drunk as he lurched into the center of the room and searched for Jesus who had already come to his feet. Peter and his brother Andrew were already moving toward the wild man to subdue him. Seeing Jesus, the crazed intruder's high-pitched voice shrieked in a staccato babble:

"What do you want of us? What do you want of us, Jesus of Nazareth?"

He scowled, pointing at Jesus with both hands and, letting his head rear back while his eyes rolled in his head. Everyone was now on their feet and the synagogue roared with their murmuring.

Peter and Andrew were rushing to the crazed man's side when he screamed with a cracking voice: "Have you come to destroy us? I know who you are…" He leered at everyone in the room holding his outstretched hands above his head.

"You are the Holy One of God!" he said.

Jesus signaled for Peter and Andrew not to subdue the man. Striding toward him with great authority, Jesus shouted above the din: "Be quiet!" The command was so powerful everyone went silent. It was to be the first action of his ministry. Jesus whispered so loudly that everyone heard him. The breathy words came in slow cadence.

"Come out of this man!" Jesus ordered.

In that instant the man's knees buckled and he collapsed at Jesus' feet and

began to shake violently. His legs fluttered as if trying to shake off the gnawing of unseen evils. Then from the depths of his body the man bellowed in agony. The ethereal bawling unleashed rivulets of fear in the congregation who stood frozen in awe.

Jesus turned from the man at his feet and returned to his bench. Peter and Andrew helped the man to get up and escorted him outside. Those remaining sat wide-eyed staring at Jesus, wondering "Is he really the Holy one of God?"

The murmuring slowly began again and quickly rose to an excited roar as the congregation asked themselves how Jesus could command evil spirits. Truly this is a teacher with such authority as has never been seen before.

✝

This explosive revelation of Jesus' power still did not convince some of the Jews present that night in the synagogue. They still had to wonder if they were really in the presence of 'the Holy One of God.'

Even the disciples struggled with this question and later Jesus would ask of them, "Who do you say that I am?"

The revelation of Jesus in our own lives presents the same question to us. Do we live our lives in the sure knowledge that he is 'the Holy One of God?' It calls for deep reflection because later Jesus may also ask of us: "Who do you say that I am?

5th Sunday in Ordinary Time
Mark 1: 29-39

This is what I have come to do!

Simon-Peter heard voices in his dream. He was dreaming that his boat was rolling heavily in the seas and his nets were slipping over the side. The voices were warning him about the nets. Peter clutched his blanket and rolled onto his left side but the voices persisted.

Suddenly Peter opened his eyes and realized he had been dreaming. Yet, the voices were still there. "Jesus. We want to see Jesus!" they shouted.

Peter growled, throwing his blanket aside. He struggled to his feet and shuffled past the other sleepers on his way to the front door. He rubbed his eyes and face, yawned and wondered how early it was!

The red sky behind the lake was splattered with flocks of little clouds, each edged in gold on the bottom, but dark as thunder on top. The ruddy sun, just cresting the eastern hills, sent shafts of gold light to edge the anxious faces of the crowds clamoring outside Peter's house. Peter glared at them for waking him up. But his expression softened as the events last night started coming back to him.

Peter remembered how amazing it had been to see Jesus take his mother-in-law's hand and lift her up. She seemed reborn into instant health. The healings had continued into the night.

One of the Peter's fishing companions called to him from the front of the crowd. "Simon, please bring him outside. We want to see Jesus. We heard he cured your mother-in-law."

Peter didn't answer. He turned back into his house and searched the floor to see which sleeping lump was Jesus. Instead he found his mother-in-law sitting in the shadows of the room. "He left early this morning," she announced.

Peter, Andrew, James and John soon set off to find Jesus. They worked their way quickly through the narrow streets of Capernaum and out onto the fields to the west. Beyond were the foothills where they found him on a grassy knoll overlooking the lake.

Rushing up to Jesus, Peter scolded: "Everyone is looking for you!"

Jesus replied: "Let us move on to the neighboring villages so that I may proclaim the good news there also. That is what I have come to do!"

✝

When Jesus said "that is what I have come to do," he explained the purpose his incarnation: to tell of God's plan for us. Indeed, Jesus had come to proclaim the good news to the world. Raising up Peter's mother-in-law is a foreshadowing of the resurrection that is promised to all of us who believe.

Peter's mother-in-law began to serve them immediately. Her action is a foreshadowing of the call which has been given to each of us. We are called to be servants to one another. We are called to tell the world of God's plan for us.

6th sunday in Ordinary Time
Mark 1: 40-45

Be clean...

The hot Galilean sun burned down on the yellow slopes that overlooked the Sea of Galilee. Jesus and his disciples had taken refuge in the shade of a grove of trees. Hoping for a breeze from the lake, Jesus leaned back against one of the trees. Above him legions of noisy insects chattered in the branches and leaves.

"Hot, hot, hot!" Peter grumbled as he loosened his robe with one hand and fanned his face with the other. They were still more than an hour's walk from Capernaum and it was too hot to go further.

Peter eyed the road below them as it snaked northward. Jesus was looking in the other direction along the way they had just come. The lone man who had been following them all morning was getting closer. Peter noticed Jesus looking south along the road and propped himself up on one elbow to see what Jesus was seeing.

The man seemed to be hobbling as if he had an injured foot, but his pace was steady. He held his head high, scanning ahead to see where Jesus and his disciples had gone. When he reached the point on the road just below the grove of trees he looked up, squinting against the brilliant light. When the man saw the disciples sitting together in the dark shade he began to climb toward them.

Jesus watched the man struggle up the hill. When he was close enough for all to see that he was an unclean leper, the disciples began to move away from him. He stopped directly in front of Jesus, gasping for breath. His beard covering cloth and his ragged, dirty robe told of his long struggle with disease.

 Jesus remained seated as the leper boldly stepped closer to him and then kneeled before him in a gesture of reverence. Jesus looked at the man with pity. His face and arms were pocked with scales and scabs.

He looked into Jesus' eyes and pleaded: "If you will to do so, you can cure me."

Without hesitation Jesus reached out and put his fingertips directly on the man's sores. "I do will it. Be cured."

Peter watched in amazement as the man's skin cleared. The marks and rashes simply dissolved.

A breeze scurried up the hillside billowing the tall yellow grass and sending a breath of coolness into the grove.

✝

Confident faith in Jesus' healing power is frequently the pre-requisite of a cure. In ancient superstition such skin diseases were considered to be caused by devils who must be expelled. Until this was done the diseased person was not clean and could therefore not enter the temple.

Today as the penitential season of Lent approaches we are challenged to carry our banner of confident faith in Jesus' healing power.

7th Sunday in Ordinary Time
Mark 2: 1-12

Pick up your mat and go home...

Little chunks of dried mud showered down on Jesus head. He looked up at the ceiling and saw a hand come through. The hand gripped the thatches that formed the roof and pulled them away from the heavy roof beams. A shaft of light streamed down through the opening.

Peter's house was packed with people who had crowded in to hear Jesus. The yard outside was full of people. The street was full of people. For days there had been nothing but people.

Those in the room with Jesus stood in astonished silence looking up as two faces peered down through the gaping hole. Peter sputtered, unable to find words to shout at the men on his roof who were tearing away more thatching to make the hole larger.

The room briefly darkened as four men lowered a stretcher down through the hole. The crowd backed up to give room for the man descending into their midst. He lay helpless and twisted on his pallet. Looking for the one they call Jesus, his frightened eyes searched the faces circled above him,

Jesus was still looking up at the four hopeful men who stood on the roof, peering down through the hole. Jesus smiled up at them, pleased with their faith and amused at the lengths they had gone to get the paralyzed man into the room.

As Jesus lowered his eyes to the man lying on the pallet before him, he caught sight of Peter. The fisherman was looking at him glumly. With a brief smile and a cock of his head Jesus wordlessly assured Peter that the roof of his house could be repaired

The crippled man recognized Jesus and tried to reach up to him. Powerfully moved by this demonstration of faith, Jesus declared in a loud voice: "My son, your sins are forgiven."

One of the scribes smirked at his friend.

As if to drive such doubt away, Jesus almost shouted at the paralyzed man before him.

"I command you: Stand up! Pick up your mat and go home."

The light pouring through the roof hole streamed down on the cripple who lifted himself up on one elbow, then rolled onto his side and brought his legs up and rolled again until he was on his hands and knees. He did not hesitate, coming to a crouching position and then standing up strong and straight. His eyes danced with excitement and he held his hands out for balance. The man turned to Jesus and tried to speak but too much emotion left him voiceless.

Jesus glanced down at the empty stretcher. The man remembered the command and bent down to pick it up. He rolled the mat around the two poles and in reverent silence began to make his way to the door.

✝

We are blessed to find our loving God always present to us. We are invited to be in "the room" with him. When our faith is weak we may find ourselves somewhere else. We end up outside. We may even be out of town!

Today's Gospel reminds up that we need to demonstrate the faith of the paralytic and his four friends. We need to come home by any means. We need to place ourselves in Jesus' presence again, even if we have to tear off the roof!

8th Sunday in Ordinary Time
Mark 2: 18-22

Poured into
new wineskins...

The people were already beginning to gather outside the synagogue in anticipation of Jesus' arrival. Josiah had closed his shop earlier than usual and walked the few blocks to Capernaum's synagogue. As Josiah was finding a seat on the ledge of the wall around the building, he was joined by his friend Asher.

"Have a seat here by me," Josiah said with a wide grin of greeting.

Asher was frowning. "I'm going to ask him questions tonight. If he's a

Jew why doesn't he act like one? He eats with tax collectors and whores. He and his disciples do anything they want. They don't fast. They haven't observed our traditions."

Josiah reflected on Asher's protest. He was proud of the traditions of the Jews. Their lives were marked with outward signs of their faith—fasting, sacrifice, circumcision, Sabbath and the law.

"Perhaps Jesus is bringing something new, something different," Josiah said. "He is a prophet. He has healed many. How can you explain that?"

"I can't explain it," Asher said, staring into his empty hands.

The crowd began to cheer as they caught sight of Jesus and his disciples coming toward them. When Jesus took his place on the top steps of the synagogue, Asher fired off his first question about fasting.

Jesus took no offense at Asher's abrupt challenge. Instead, he was smiling as he answered with a question of his own.

"How can the guests at a wedding fast as long as the groom is still among them? So long as the groom stays with them they cannot fast."

Wedding feasts sometimes lasted a week and Jesus' words seemed to answer Asher's challenge but posed new questions.

Jesus continued, "The day will come, however, when the groom will be taken away from them; on that day they will fast."

"I think Jesus is bringing us a change," Josiah said. "He brings us something new!"

Asher wasn't ready for any change. "He's bringing us trouble," he grumbled.

Jesus continued his answer with more examples.

"No-one sews a patch of unshrunken cloth on an old cloak. If he should do so, the very thing he has used to cover the hole would pull away—the new from the old—and the tear would get worse."

Asher turned to Josiah. "We don't need a patch. We have the law. We have our God. Our faith is strong."

Jesus went on. "No man pours new wine into old wineskins. If he does so, the wine will burst the skins and both the skins and the wine will be lost. No, new wine is poured into new wineskins."

Despite Asher's doubts, Josiah felt inspired by Jesus. He saw himself as one of the new wineskins ready to receive the new wine, the teachings of Jesus.

✞

Jesus makes all things new. When we are filled with the new wine of faith we must become new wineskins. Just as the disciples left their old life in order to follow Jesus into a new life, we must make a similar decision. When we do, we begin the journey that leads us to the threshold of paradise where we enter into our new, eternal life

9th Sunday in Ordinary Time
Mark 2: 23—3-6

'The Lord of the Sabbath'

The tall grain moved under the press of the wind, changing color as it billowed in the sunlight. Against the yellow background of the fields and the hills beyond, the figure of a white-robed man was moving north on the Capernaum Road.

Fired by a raging anger, Jesus was walking at a furious pace. The disciples, unable to keep up, were now far behind.

Jesus was just as glad to be alone. He didn't want the disciples to see him in this fury. His leg muscles burned with exhaustion, but the fast walking was slowly burning off the anger. The pain was somehow cleansing.

The hot afternoon breeze whipped his robes about him, slowing his pace as he stalked on. Capernaum was still a distant smudge on the horizon where the pale land met the dark blue lake.

Peter and the others were making steady progress along the Capernaum Road, but Jesus was now out of their sight somewhere up ahead.

Peter was explaining his version of what happened. "Someone must have sent those rabbis. They'll do anything to stop Jesus."

The disciples with Peter recalled the tense exchange between Jesus and the two Pharisees who had interrupted Jesus' teaching, rising to their feet and pointing their long fingers at him.

"Look!" they said. "Why do they do a thing not permitted on the sabbath?" The outburst had taken the crowd seated on the hillside by surprise. The two rabbis looked for reactions. Everyone knew it was the sabbath day. Earlier they had all seen the disciples plucking the heads of grain. Even Jesus had eaten some.

Jesus had a look of dismay on his face. He was frustrated by their lack of understanding. He was tired of being hounded by the Pharisees with their attempts to discredit him. It was also hot and Jesus was tired.

Slowly, Jesus got to his feet and pointed back at the two rabbis. "Have you never read what David did when he was in need and he and his men were

hungry?" The rabbis had surely read the Scroll of Samuel which told the story of David and his men eating the holy bread of the priests.

While they thought of that, Jesus continued: "The Sabbath was made for man, not man for the Sabbath. That is why the Son of Man is lord even of the Sabbath."

Peter and the disciples crested a hill and far ahead in the distance they saw the white robe of Jesus. There was no hurry, they would find Jesus in the Capernaum synagogue at sundown.

"He's teaching us that good works are more important than just obeying the law!" Peter smiled at himself for his insight to say that.

In Caparnaum, an old fish buyer named Azaram sighed loudly as he stared at his gnarled left hand. It has suddenly started throbbing. His twisted fingers had been locked around his withered thumb for half a lifetime. The frozen hand was like a dead stump on the end of his arm. Azaram had long ago learned to live with it, but this new pain was something to worry about. As he headed for the synagogue for the evening prayer the pain continued to flicker through his hand. Azaram arrived at the synagogue at the same moment as Jesus who glanced down at Azaram's withered hand. Jesus smiled at the old man.

"Go ahead, you first," he said.

When Jesus said he was lord of the sabbath he invited us to be the lords of our own "sabbath." We are challenged to do more than just meet the letter of the law. Our love and our good deeds are the real foundation of our faith. Without these we have no need of a sabbath.

10th Sunday of Ordinary Time
Mark 3: 20-35

'Whoever does the will of God...'

The adolescent girls screamed with fear when they saw Jesus through the window of the house. They had been told that Jesus was possessed by the devil, that Beelzebul, the *lord of the flies* had command of him. The crowd of people were saying that Jesus was crazy and that he used demonic powers.

When the shadowy figure of Jesus appeared by the window, it terrified the girls. Jesus, looked out the window at them, standing amid the noisy crowd. He saw the girls turn quickly away.

"Look at this crowd," Jesus said to John who came to his side by the window. The crowd had grown so large it completely surrounded the house.

"We won't be able to get out of here!" John announced. Philip added his concern that there was no food in the house and he, for one, was famished.

Beyond the crowd, hurrying down the Nazareth Road, Mary and Jesus' other family members were just arriving on the scene. They had walked the half-day trip from Nazareth, hoping to get to Jesus before it was too late. Because Jesus had astounded everyone by expelling demons, people were saying he was possessed by evil. They said this made Jesus a false teacher who was misleading the people. Under the law of the land, this was a crime punishable by death. His mother, Mary, wanted to reach Jesus before the officials did. She wanted to warn him of the danger and with the help of the family persuade him to stop and come home where he belonged. But the crowd was too thick around the house and Mary couldn't get through them.

Jesus didn't see his mother at the back of the crowd, but he did see the fearful girls who tried to hide their face from his gaze. He stepped out of the house and began to preach about Satan, kingdoms and loyalties. Jesus told them that every sin will be forgiven except blasphemies against the Holy Spirit.

Soon the young girls were no longer afraid of Jesus. His words and his way had convinced them that he was not possessed by demons. They saw

that only love and gentleness were to be found in his heart.

One of the girls felt a hand on her shoulder. The man behind her said: "The mother and family of Jesus are way at the back. They want someone to tell him that they have come."

Boldly, the girl called out to Jesus who was near. "Sir, your mother and your family are outside asking for you." Others in the crowd repeated her words. Jesus turned and faced the girl. He saw she was not afraid, so he smiled and winked his reassurance to her.

Then Jesus' face became stern. "Who are my mother and my brothers?" he shouted to the crowd, letting the words mist down upon them. Taking each of them in his sweeping gaze he declared: "Whoever does the will of God is brother and sister and mother to me."

✞

Jesus' final statement is a declaration that if we do his will we are true members of his family—the Family of God. The need to belong to something is one of our strongest yearnings. We all need to love someone. In loving another person we discover that we must "give" ourselves to them. That completes the circle for then we belong to them.

These deep waters of Jesus' teaching are an invitation to explore ourselves, our lives, our loves and our faith.

11th Sunday in Ordinary Time
Mark 4: 26-34

The Kingdom of God is like

The last of the sunset was dissolving into a sky full of stars. Jesus sat on flat stone bench and felt the heat of the summer day still rising from the rock. A cool breeze came in off the lake and Jesus sighed with contentment.

Philip asked him: "Today, you were teaching in parables. I understand the story, like the growing seeds, but what is the real meaning."

Jesus smiled at Philip and explained, "Each one must discover the meaning for themselves. The Parable of the Growing Seed teaches that these seeds are all in God's care. We may be able to plant the seeds in the ground and water them, but the seeds only grow and become what God has willed."

The other disciples in the patio listened carefully to the starlit figure sitting on the bench.

Jesus continued: "We can only stand aside and watch with wonder as the Father's power is revealed. Then, in the fullness of time, when the fields are ready and the vines and branches are ready to harvest, the Father gives us his gift. We receive all of the crop. He holds nothing back."

The disciples sat in silence with Jesus under the canopy of stars. No-one spoke. They were thinking about seeds.

Andrew suddenly declared: "Then you are such a seed...becoming what your Father has willed."

Jesus smiled again, pleased with Andrew's insight. Andrew was the first disciple, having been a follower of John the Baptist and a witness at Jesus' baptism.

Jesus said to Andrew, "You too are such a seed. And as you begin to grow this day, you cannot imagine the harvest you will bring. I assure you, it will be so great that, like the yield of the mustard seed, the birds of the air will make their nest in your branches."

The Disciples sat again in reflective silence. A scent of smoke passed by on the gentle breeze. Two dogs were barking in the distance. The stars brightened in the darkening sky. It had been a long day. Peter yawned and got up to go into the house.

Jesus closed his eyes and rested. It was too dark for anyone to see that he was still smiling. It had been a very good day.

✝

    Jesus and his small band of disciples were themselves like a tiny mustard seed. The vast Roman Empire sprawled over the Mediterranean world. They were just a few insignificant fishermen from one of the primitive territories of the empire. They had no rank or title. Yet the Jews believed that God would one day establish his kingdom to rule unchallenged over all the earth. How then could the future glory of such a kingdom be contained in the obscure carpenter's son who came down to Galilee to begin his ministry?

    How then can the kingdom of God be contained in each one of us? God will provide the power for the seeds to grow in our heart if we are willing to nourish them with the water of our love and faith.

12th Sunday in Ordinary Time
Mark 4: 35-41

Night Crossing

It had been a tiring day.

Jesus and the disciples had been teaching to the crowds gathered along the lakeside near Capernaum where Peter lived. Some of the disciples had already waded out to climb into the heavy workboats, bobbing and tugging at their lines. The sun had just set behind the hilly horizon as Jesus approached the boats. As he waded toward the nearest boat, the coolness of the water eased his tired feet.

"Let's cross over to the other side during the night," Jesus said, as he climbed up over the gunnels of the boat. In the gathering dusk they cast off from the shore and pulled out into the darkening waters of the Sea of Galilee.

Exhausted from the day, Jesus went to the sheltered bench at the stern of the boat and was soon fast asleep. In the gathering storm clouds and rising wind, the boat was soon dipping low and scooping up the tops of the higher waves. The heavy bow bashed into the breakers and the roaring wind blasted the spray back into the boat. the violence of the storm was quickly beyond the limit of the boat. The disciples were awash in the water up to their knees and they began to bail. One of the drenched disciples stopped and worked his way to the stern of the boat where Jesus was still asleep. Screaming above the roar of the wind, the disciple woke Jesus, pleading for him to save them.

Jesus rose and surveyed the wind which lifted his hair away from his head. He raised his arms and shouted into the gale: "Be still..."

In that instant the wind stopped; the sea fell flat. Clouds dissolved and shafts of moonlight streamed down onto the motionless boat in the midst of the black sea. The eerie silence was broken only by the after-drip of water as the disciples stared at Jesus in amazement.

☦

The same Jesus that stilled the sea 2000 years ago is aboard each of our lives today. He can still the storms in our life. We need only to call out in faith to know his presence and power in our lives.

13th Sunday of Ordinary Time
Mark 5: 21-43

'Talitha Koum'

Jesus waded ashore, enjoying the cool water on his feet. When he looked up he saw a well-dressed man running toward him. Higher up on the shore a large crowd was waiting

"It's Jairus," Peter said, wading in behind Jesus. Jairus was the prominent leader of Peter's synagogue at Capernaum, and when he dropped to his knees and fell at Jesus' feet the crowd gasped. Such homage should be reserved for God alone.

Jairus was a frightened man. His wet eyes were red with exhaustion. "My little daughter is critically ill. Please come and lay your hands on her so that she may get well and live," he begged.

They started off to Jairus' house and the crowd followed. As they went a woman from the crowd scurried up behind Jesus and reached out to touch his robe, knowing that his magic was strong enough to cure her bleeding. Jesus felt power leave him and turned to find the one who had drawn it. The woman came forward and Jesus told her that his healing power first required her faith.

"Daughter, it is your faith that has healed you." he said.

As Jesus, Jairus and the crowd continued toward the house, messengers arrived. By their expressions Jairus knew it was too late.

"Your daughter is dead," they told him. Jairus buried his face in his hands and began to sob. Jesus put his hand on Jairus and told him: "Fear is useless, what is needed is trust." Jairus had declared his complete faith and trust when he prostrated himself before Jesus at the shore. Realizing this, they hurried on.

When they arrived at Jairus' house there were many mourners making a loud din with their wailing voices. Jesus ordered them out and with only Jairus, his wife, and three disciples, Peter, James and John, Jesus entered the girl's room. She lay motionless on the bed. Everyone grew silent in expectation and little shivers of fear raced through their minds and they gave the moment over to the healer's power. Jesus stood silently, looking over at the girl. Peter looked up at Jesus' face and saw him tighten his jaw as if summoning power.

Jesus walked up to the bed and knelt down, bending close to her. Then he softly said in his Aramaic language: "Talitha koum, Little girl, get up.."

Her eyes fluttered open and she obeyed, getting up and beginning to walk around the room. Jesus rose to his feet, stepped back and smiled broadly. He looked over at Jairus whose face could find no way to simultaneously express his many emotions. His shock, joy and gratitude came out as a teary-eyed grin. Jairus' wife stood in a trance. Jesus went to her and said, "Why don't you get your daughter something to eat? She must be hungry."

✞

All people are hungry for healings in their lives. Some who have fallen in their faith may long to hear Jesus' call to "get up" In these two stories we are taught that such healings and risings are possible only if we have faith and confidence in Jesus. His power and our faith combine to effect the miracles. On the last day of our lives when we close our eyes to this world it will be the faith that we have lived that will enable us to hear Jesus' invitation: "Talitha koum, rise up." When he calls our faith will open our eyes to his paradise and the many mansions that he has prepared for us.

14th Sunday of Ordinary Time
Mark 6: 1-6

Nazareth...

Jesus and his Disciples paused at the crest of the Tiberias Road. From the ridge they could look down on the white houses of Nazareth which stair-stepped down the slopes to the bottom of the Valley of Esdraelon. The rooftops were edged with gold reflections from the setting sun.

Jesus sighed, feeling a little fearful about returning to his home town. He and the disciples had been walking since midmorning, climbing the foothills from Tiberias. Tired, thirsty and hungry, they were eager to make the final descent down the footpaths into Nazareth where they would be welcomed in Jesus home. Hurrying to beat the darkness, they started down.

When Jesus opened the door to his house, Mary was overjoyed at his unexpected return and jumped to her feet, rushing to embrace him. After hugging him she opened her eyes and noticed that he had brought an invasion of hungry men with him. The disciples smiled sheepishly as they crowded into the small house.

The next day was the Sabbath and Jesus took his friends with him to the synagogue. When Jesus rose to speak, everyone grew silent, waiting to see what the carpenter's son would have to say. He held them spellbound as he preached. His words thundered with authority. His stories were like perfectly cut stones which connected with other parables to build a foundation for his teachings.

The following day the whole village of Nazareth seemed to be talking about Jesus. The disciples heard the gossip, asking how an ordinary Nazarean carpenter had any business preaching in their synagogue.

"What are they saying about me?" Jesus asked.

Peter looked away and did not answer.

"What?" Jesus demanded.

"They don't believe in you." Philip blurted.

Jesus looked down at his feet. He knew Mary's eyes were on him. His own town was rejecting him. His confidence flowed out of him, like wine from a punctured skin.

"No prophet is without honor," Jesus said to them, looking directly at his

mother, "except in his native place, among his own kindred, and in his own house."

Mary's eyes grew moist with sad tears as she looked at her poor son. Jesus' eyes glistened back. They both knew this would be the last time they would ever be home together. In the morning Mary would close the door behind him and Jesus would never return home again.

✝

There comes a time in each of our lives when we realize that "we can't go home again." We may return to the place, but the home of our childhood is no longer there. It is changed by time and will never be the same again.

There also comes a time in our lives when we must make the decision to give ourselves back to God. When we pledge our lives to follow Jesus, we become his disciples. We can never return to be who we once were. We will have become new creatures who walk in newness of life.

Two by two

Jesus put his arms around Peter and Andrew and guided them up to the road. The two brothers carried only long walking sticks as they headed out, empty-handed and full of fear.

Peter looked at Jesus with pleading in his eyes: "I'm just a fisherman, Lord..."

"And a good one, too!" Jesus reassured, "but you are also a fisher of men. You can do this as well. You have the power and authority. Believe me!"

Both of them knew they must go on this mission into the towns and villages of Galilee. Jesus was sending them with instructions to take nothing with them. They would soon discover God's strength in their weakness.

Pausing at the road, Andrew and Peter turned to face Jesus. "Remember this," Jesus said. "You have the authority over unclean spirits. Preach repentance." They had heard these words of repentance which John the Baptist had preached. During the previous months they had learned from Jesus—by his preaching and by his example. Now, as the first disciples chosen by Jesus, they were the first being sent out alone.

"Jesus, we have nothing with us, no food, no coins, not even water to drink." Peter protested in a last, desperate appeal to reason.

Jesus answered with a patient smile. His eyes told Peter and Andrew that this was a test of their faith. If they truly believed that God would provide for them, then the first demons they must expel are their own demons of fear and doubt.

Jesus hugged them strongly, clapping their backs with his hands as if to pack down the fullest measure of his confidence in them.

Once Peter and Andrew had set out, the road that stretched before them was the familiar route that led south toward Tiberias. Beyond that were the villages.

They heard the noisy morning chatter of birds perched in the trees fronting the lake. Bright sunlight was dancing in the sky. It was a glorious morning and the sweetness of life was upon them. Peter jabbed his walking

stick into the ground ahead and Andrew echoed a rhythmic double tap with his own stick. Peter got the joke and they both began to laugh.

✝

If Peter and Andrew come to our house will we welcome them in? Will we give them food and water to drink, wash their tunics and give them a bed in which to sleep? Will we allow them to stay as long as they want?

Or have we already sent them away, causing them to shake our dust from their feet? Somehow these questions challenge us to examine the depth of our faith and commitment to being a follower of Jesus Christ.

16th Sunday of Ordinary Time
Mark 6: 30-34

The resting place

J esus took off his sandals and holding them in his hand he waded into the water. The refreshing coolness soothed his tired feet.

The Sea of Galilee stretched before him, a band of blue beneath the sweltering hills on the other side. To the north the shoreline curved away toward green clumps of trees on a distant headland. A breeze ruffled the water and flowed across Jesus' hot face. The cool air was like the Father's caress, affirming him and all that he had accomplished in the past hectic weeks.

The Disciples were now returned from their first two-by-two journeys into neighboring towns and villages. They all had miraculous stories to tell to Jesus. Even now Peter was rambling on about his preaching, anointing and healing experiences. Jesus felt proud of his brave disciples. They had been so full of faith as they went without him into the harsh world.

Suddenly a sad awareness surged through Jesus. It came like a dark shadow passing overhead. He realized that his disciples' first practice mission was a real preparation for what they must soon do without him. It was all happening so fast. If only time could stand still...if only...

The noise of the approaching crowd stirred Jesus from these thoughts and he turned from the tranquil solitude of the lake to face them. Like a thick syrup, the crowd flowed down the hillsides to the water's edge. There were thousands of them. Like a great flock of sheep they patiently waited with their shepherd. Jesus' only escape was by boat, out onto the water. John and the other Disciples had been sent to get a boat. They were now sculling a beamy fishboat along the shoreline. When they reached Jesus Andrew tossed a line to Peter who hauled the stern into shallow water. Jesus and Peter climbed into the boat and the others began to row out against the breeze.

They followed the coastline, hoping to find a deserted place where they could put ashore and rest a little. The afternoon breeze shifted south, so they raised a sail and began to glide silently toward the north shore. The sun rolled westward over the Galilean Hills and began to fall toward the horizon and behind the cities of Merom and Hazor which lay beyond it.

They lowered their sail as the boat rounded a tree-covered headland and

they rowed into the sheltered bay hidden behind it. It wasn't deserted. People were already there, waiting. They had followed on foot.

Jesus sighed. There would be no rest. These were his people, his followers, his flock. He would give them everything. Now it was only his energy. Later it would be his life.

Jesus waded ashore, shedding his exhaustion like water. He began to preach.

☦

All of us have experienced complete exhaustion. We have reached the end of our road; we're at the limits of our ability to cope. It seems impossible to go on. Yet, we must go on, and we do, in the face of everything we somehow survive. In moments like these we live our finest hour. We triumph.

If we can hold firm to the deep-rooted tree of our faith, when we one day encounter mighty storms from the gates of hell, these torrents and winds shall not prevail against us. Holding on, no matter what, we shall triumph.

17th Sunday of Ordinary Time
John 6: 1-15

In the sharing

Jesus looked down at the five loaves of bread and two small fish which the disciples had brought before him. The loaves were stuffed into a basket with their golden brown ends promising a satisfying crust. The two fish looked forlorn lying in the bottom of the woven basket.

On the grassy hillside the people sat in long rows watching expectantly as Jesus and his disciples talked the situation over. The disciples stepped back, leaving Jesus the center of attention.

Slowly Jesus raised his eyes heavenward and lifted the bread and the fish up in an offering. Those close enough saw Jesus lips move in silent prayer. The evening breeze coming in off the lake rippled the long, dark hair which framed Jesus' face. With a brightness in his eyes, Jesus lowered the baskets of bread and fish and set them down.

He withdrew the first loaf and broke it in half, handing the large hunk to Peter. As he took the bread, Peter saw the other half of the loaf in Jesus' hand still whole and unbroken. When Peter looked again at his own half of the loaf, it too was whole and unbroken. He gasped and looked questioningly into Jesus' face. When their eyes met, Peter's held the question, "Is this a miracle?" and the answer was in his own hand. Jesus' eyes warmed when he smiled back in reassurance. Peter was indeed part of the miracle that was happening. He beamed in joy and tore his new loaf in half and held two full loaves. Peter began passing the golden loaves into the outstretched hands of the multitudes.

✞

In this famous miracle of Jesus we discover our loving God, who will not let us go hungry. This is the same God who sets the stars in place and builds this beautiful world in which we live. It is the God of all creation who still takes time to distribute bread and fish to his faithful creatures. Such love.

We can work our own miracles of the loaves and fishes by distributing our love to the world around us. Each of our gifts of love will leave us with more love than we can ever give. We can never run out of love as long as we keep giving it away.

18th Sunday of Ordinary Time
John 6:24-35

The bread of life

The boats from Tiberias were crowded with passengers which they were carrying back to Capernaum. Behind them was the beach where the boatmen had noticed the crowds, clamoring for a ride to the other side of the lake. Their fares exceeded what the boatmen could have made from fishing for the day, and it was an easy run because the sea was remarkably calm after the sudden storm which had raged the waters during the night.

The boat was full of talk about Jesus and the miracle of the loaves. The young boy standing by the fat helmsman boasted, "I am the one that brought the five barley loaves and the two fish."

The helmsman steered off course for a moment as he looked down at the lad. "And that was enough to feed all of these people and those still on the shore?" he laughed.

The others in the boat began to compare Jesus with Moses who had given the people bread from heaven. One man exclaimed: "Surely Jesus is a new Moses who has the power to challenge not only the kings of Israel but the power of Rome itself." Everyone agreed that Jesus was a new king, a new leader for the people.

When they reached Capernaum they were astounded to learn that Jesus was already there. He had not left with his disciples on the only boat the night before. Yet, here he was.

It was then that Jesus told the crowds that they were wrongly seeking him for earthly food. He told them he was the living bread. "I am the bread of life. He who comes to me will never be hungry; he who believes in me will never thirst."

The young boy who had brought the loaves and fishes the day before went straight to Jesus and stood by his side. He looked up with admiration at the tall teacher beside him. Jesus recognized the boy and smiled down, placing his hand on the boy's shoulder. Jesus hugged him to his side and repeated what he had just said: "I am the bread of life. He who comes to me shall not hunger; and he who believes in me shall never thirst."

✝

Today's Gospel challenges us to examine the depth of our faith. Do we come to Mass every Sunday just for our satisfaction...a "free meal" at Communion. Or are we there because of the strength of our faith. We believe.

Who are we in this crowd of Sunday followers. Are we those seeking only for today, or are we the ones who know the truth of Jesus' words: "...believe in the One God sent."

19th Sunday in Ordinary Time
John 6: 41-51

Bread from heaven

Peter took a protective step toward Jesus' and ran his burly fingers up through his beard and over the top of his head. The Synagogue at Capernaum was filled with loud voices protesting the claim of Jesus that he was the living bread come down from heaven.The argument would have gone on a long time, but fortunately it was getting late and many were already leaving for their homes.

Peter leaned close to Jesus speaking softly. "I don't understand what you're saying," he said, offering a sheepish smile. "Tell me again?"

Jesus looked away, waiting for more patience to come and numb the situation. He took a deep breath and studied Peter's hopeful face.

"I am the living bread that came down from heaven," Jesus repeated. He patiently reminded Peter that the Lord had told Moses he would rain down bread from heaven to feed the starving Israelites. Jesus said in the same way he was sent by the Father to offer eternal life to those who believed and followed him.

Peter sat down on the bench to let the words soak in. He lapsed into silence, looking at the floor and slowly massaging his fingers.

"Everyone else has gone home," Jesus noted. Looking over at Peter, he asked, "Shall we leave now?"

Peter nodded and they both headed for the door. Outside the half moon was sprinkling shards of silver on the waters of the lake. They breathed deep, filling themselves with the perfect night air. It was too beautiful a night to waste in sleep, but they were both tired. Jesus put his arm around Peter's shoulder and gave him a reassuring clap on the back.

"Think about it some more, Peter. Your heart already knows these things. I've just put them into words for your ears." Jesus said.

"I believe, Lord." Peter said with all his heart. "I'll go home and sleep on it."

Jesus smiled warmly. "Okay, let's both do that."

Peter turned and headed toward his small house. Jesus looked up into the

night sky, beyond the stars, beyond time. The night's teaching at the synagogue, the grumbling men, and the barrage of questions had been exhausting. He was suddenly very tired. An unexpected breeze chattered through the trees and in the rustling of the leaves Jesus thought he heard a voice say, "Sleep now, my son. Sleep well."

✝

Jesus is the bread of life. In Eucharist we receive him and the promise of eternal life which he preached. Such a fine gift: bread to sustain us on our daily life journey and at the end of this life we receive welcome to cross the threshold of eternity and walk with God.

20th Sunday in Ordinary Time
John 6:51-58

The bread of eternal life!

The synagogue at Capernaum echoed with angry voices. Some of the Jews, appalled at Jesus' wild assertions, were trying to argue on the side of reason. Other Jews were telling their stories of the miracles of Jesus. And in the midst of this din, Jesus sat, like an accused prisoner, listening to them drag his ministry back and forth in the dispute.

An old man with gray eyes and a gray beard rose to his feet. Stabbing at the sky with a warning finger, he shouted, "How can this man give us his flesh to eat?" He then pointed at Jesus, standing nearby. His eyes flared with indignation.

"He claims to be living bread from heaven. I see only Jesus of Nazareth. I see only a wanderer, one expelled from his own town. He is not Moses. He is not Elijah," the old man railed.

Jesus moved toward his accuser. His eyes searched the old man's face, looking for a point of contact: "Truly, truly, I say to you, if you do not eat the flesh of the Son of Man and drink his blood you have no life in you. He who feeds on my flesh and drinks my blood has life eternal, and I will raise him up on the last day."

The Jews in the synagogue all began to talk at once. They couldn't comprehend that Jesus had come from God. It was unthinkable that the man in their midst was Yahweh.

Jesus' heart went out to them as they thrashed in the tank of their small world. They could not know that millions of people down through the centuries would indeed eat his flesh and drink his blood. They could not know that Jesus himself would be the sacrifice, given up for them.

Jesus wanted to leave the synagogue and escape into the solitude of the hills above Capernaum. Instead, he stayed, sitting with his disciples and patiently facing their angry eyes.

✝

    Jesus must have felt overwhelmed with rejection as he tried to teach the uncomprehending world who he is. The world could not accept him. His miracles drew vast crowds of believers one day but the next day he was ridiculed. Even his own disciples faltered in their attempt at faith. At times the hopelessness of Jesus' ministry must have been unbearable for him.

    Even today it seems incomprehensible that God would choose to live among us as Jesus. But his love and the truth is the impossible. We can only walk by faith and only then will we know the truth.

21st Sunday in Ordinary Time
John 6: 60-69

And you?
Do you believe?

Jesus and his disciples left the synagogue at Capernaum and headed for Peter's house. It was time for the evening meal and everyone was tired. Jesus, himself, looked very small and very alone as he walked in their midst. His sandaled feet marked a thoughtful cadence as they strode along. It had been painful for Jesus to listen to the Jews challenge his claim that by eating his flesh and drinking his blood they would come to eternal life. The teaching did, in fact, sound preposterous to them. Despite his explanations, they still rejected him.

And now, as they walked, Jesus heard his own disciples arguing about this teaching.

As they neared the house, Jesus stopped and faced his followers. "And you, do you believe?" he asked them.

Trying to avoid a direct answer, Andrew said: "This is a hard saying. It is a teaching that we cannot understand. How can anyone believe it?"

"Does it shake your faith, Andrew?" Jesus asked, his eyes extending the question to each of the disciples.

When no-one spoke, Jesus continued, "What then if you were to see the Son of Man ascend to where he was before...?"

They continued to look at him in silence.

Jesus went on: "It is the spirit that gives life; the flesh is useless. The words I spoke to you are spirit and life. Yet among you there are some who do not believe."

Judas shifted his weight to the other foot.

"That is why I have told you," Jesus said, "that no one can come to me unless it is granted him by the Father."

Some of the disciples slipped away in the darkness; the rest stood silent-

ly. Jesus asked them directly: "Do you want to leave me too?"

Peter answered him, speaking for the remaining disciples. "Lord, to whom shall we go? You have the words of eternal life. We have come to believe; we are convinced that you are God's holy one."

✝

In our daily journey as Christians we are constantly called to reaffirm our belief. The modern world doesn't make it easy to be a Christian; it tempts us to turn our back on our faith. "Seriously, don't tell me you believe in all that?" they ask, hoping we will join them in their smug security.

If Jesus were to ask 'Do you want to leave me too?" what would you say? If he were to ask "Do you believe?" how would you answer?

22nd Sunday in Ordinary Time
Mark 7: 1-8, 14-15, 21-23

Declaring the truth

The Disciples Thaddeus and Bartholomew watched Jesus with admiration as he rose to his feet and stalked the two visiting Pharisees from Jerusalem. The two specialists in Jewish law were bearded, gray and thick-lipped. The oldest religious lawyer looked like a pouting child—about to cry. Jesus snarled at them, calling them hypocrites.

The Pharisees had just charged that Jesus and his followers were unclean because they did not follow the Jewish ritual of meticulous washing before eating.

Thaddeus grinned as Jesus took the words of the Prophet Isaiah and easily trapped the Pharisees within them: "This people honors me with their lips, but their heart is far from me..."

The disciples had seen this fierce side of Jesus appear every time the Pharisees tried to trap him in the details of the Jewish laws. Each time this occurred Jesus would overturn their tables and drive them into sputtering helplessness by his brilliant logic and eloquent speech.

Boldly turning to the crowd, Jesus asked them: "Then are you also without understanding?" The little jab at the Pharisees raised some eyebrows. Bartholomew underscored it by nudging Thaddeus in the ribs.

Jesus continued, "Nothing that enters a man from outside can make him impure; that which comes out of him, and only that, constitutes impurity."

Like punished children, the Pharisees sat voicelessly, as Jesus moved his retort to a stunning conclusion. He raised a hand, as if to signal the key point, and smiled at the crowd. They hung by his words, suspended in rapt attention, like thirsty travelers about to receive water.

"Wicked designs come from the deep recesses of the heart; acts of fornication, theft, murder, adulterous conduct, greed, maliciousness, deceit, sensuality, envy, blasphemy, arrogance—all these evils come from within and render a man impure. What comes out of a person is what defiles that person," Jesus declared.

"For from within, out of the heart of one, come evil thoughts, fornication, theft, murder, adultery, coveting, wickedness, deceit, licentiousness, envy,

slander, pride, and foolishness." Jesus paused, allowing them time to realize their own acquaintance with these evils. Thaddeus and Bartholomew each remembered their own times when evil had come from their hearts.

Jesus underscored his teaching, saying: "All these evil things come from within, and they defile one."

The people and the Pharisees silently reflected on this new teaching. Jesus was absolutely right!

✝

Many of us may be able to identify with the Pharisees. The "Lip service" they were accused of sounds like how we may sometimes come to Mass out of habit: bringing our bodies but leaving our hearts at home.

Jesus' powerful point, that a defiling evil does not come from outside, but is born inside our hearts, invites us to consider the discipline that is necessary to cultivate a heart that is pure.

Our Christianity invites us to follow Jesus by standing up to the Pharisees of our Time— by courageously declaring the Truth in our lives.

23rd Sunday in Ordinary Time
Mark 7: 31-37

'Nnn~ma, Djuh, Djuh!'

Jesus' travels had taken him out of Jewish territory into the northern communities of the gentiles, the pagans. Even there, the stories of his healing power were known. As he entered one of the ten villages on the shores of the Lake of Galilee, a group of men were hurrying toward him. In front was a man about Jesus' age. He started to run, holding his arms up in prayerful supplication.

"Nnn-ma, Djuh, Djuh," the man strained to speak, bringing his hopeful face so close that Jesus could smell his breath.

His friends filled in around them, explaining, "He is deaf and cannot speak clearly. He begs you to heal him." The deaf man's eyes were fervent with hope.

Nearly all of Jesus' miracles had been performed among his own Jewish community. To heal this man, who was not a Jew, would emphasize that Jesus' message and preaching were for all people, not just the Jews. Yet, the revelation that he was the Messiah was for his disciples only, and even then he was revealing it by very slow degrees.

The crowd now forming wanted to see the magician do his trick right there in front of them. Jesus, needed to have intimacy with his Father. So he decided to take the man aside and heal him privately. He led the jabbering deaf man away from the crowd. When alone, Jesus cradled the mans head in his hands and pushed his index fingers into the man's ears—as if he was opening a passageway into them.

"Nnn-ma, Djuh, Djuh," the man stammered again, his eyes wild with excitement. His whole body began to tremble.

Jesus lifted his eyes heavenward and gave up a loud groan. "Be opened," he commanded in a stern voice, still holding the man's head in his hands. Like water bursting through a broken dam, sound flooded the man's ears as he heard Jesus cry out, "Ephphatha!"

Jesus spat and touched the man's tongue, releasing the impediment.

The words he had been trying to say burst free on his tongue with crystal clarity. 'Heal me, Jesus," he said.

Jesus smiled at him. "You are healed. But I ask you not to tell anyone about this."

When they returned to the waiting crowd, the man could not contain his joy. He shouted to them. "I am healed. I can speak. Jesus has given me voice and now I hear!"

Shrieks and shouts of amazement shot through the crowd as they saw the miracle before them. They began to clamor around Jesus, some with tears in their eyes. Jesus was carried along in the midst of the crowd as it flowed down the hill toward the village.

There was no escape from them. As they were swept along, like two prisoners, Jesus and the healed man exchanged glances. Despite the joy of his new hearing and speech, the man turned away from Jesus, his eyes were filled with shame. The once-deaf man realized he had failed to do the only thing that Jesus had asked of him.

✝

Has Jesus performed a miracle in your life? All of us have prayed for a special intention. Unlike the man in the Gospel story we are not asked to "tell no-one about this."

Instead we are invited to go out and preach to all nations, telling them about the good news of Jesus. This news is revealed in Scripture and in our own lives. When your prayers are answered it is God's love for you revealed. When there is a miracle in your life it is a continuation of the Gospel.

Go tell the world!

24th Sunday of Ordinary Time
Mark 8: 27-35

'Follow in my footsteps.'

Nicodemus motioned his approval to one of his staff. The man produced a pouch tied with a leather cord at the top. He counted out the coins which the spice merchant snapped up one by one until the full amount was paid. The bags and jars of spices, which Nicodemus had just purchased, were a lavish gesture of his devotion to Jesus. It took three men to carry it all.

In death Jesus would have the best that Nicodemus' money could buy, and as a rabbi, he would, himself, quietly preside at Jesus' burial.

Sundown was fast approaching, and with it the beginning of the Sabbath. With his helpers carrying the load of spices, Nicodemus led the way to the garden where he had agreed to meet Joseph of Arimathea. Joseph had offered his own tomb for the body of Jesus.

As they hurried through the streets leading out of Jerusalem, Nicodemus began to remember his secret night meetings with Jesus. Because of his high position as a rabbi, a Pharisee and a member of the Sanhedrin, he could not afford to be caught meeting with a man like Jesus. Because of his preaching, Jesus was officially opposed by the government. Nicodemus was part of the government, but he was also drawn to Jesus, and now in this bold act was beginning to take up his own cross and follow Jesus.

He remembered the night Jesus explained that to him: "Just as Moses lifted up the serpent in the desert, so must the Son of Man be lifted up so that all may believe in him." And then Jesus had said, "If you want to follow me, you will have to deny your very self and take up your own cross and follow in my footsteps."

Wide-eyed, Nicodemus imagined himself on a cross, being lifted up with the centurions straining under his weight.

The four men passed through the gate and headed outside the city. In his mind, Nicodemus could see Jesus' face before him, his eyes burning as he spoke:

"God so loved the world that he gave his only Son, that whoever believes in him may not die but may have eternal life."

Nicodemus could now see that God had given up his only Son. The sac-

rifice was real. The message was real. There was no denying it. All that remained was for Nicodemus to declare that he believed in Jesus.

"I do!" he blurted aloud.

One of the men carrying the spices, thought Nicodemus had called out to him. He ran to walk at his side.

"What did you say, sir?"

Nicodemus could only shake his head.

"Nothing."

He was not yet ready to take up his cross for Jesus. It was too dangerous. The price would be too great. He would have to deny himself and give up everything. He had too much to lose.

To truly follow Jesus he would have to become a Christian. Nicodemus knew in his heart that he already was a Christian and that he would soon reconcile this new faith with his action. He would deny his very self and take up his own cross to follow in Jesus' footsteps.

✝

Jesus asked a lot of those who wanted to follow him. Leave your boats and come. Sell what you have and give it to the poor and come. He had a way of afflicting the comfortable. The rich and powerful, like Nicodemus, had to be willing to join the poor in order to find their way into eternal life. It was hard to do.

The same applies to us. Christianity is not a warm-fuzzy, it's a hard job. It requires us to move away from the couch and into the community.

25th Sunday of the Year
Mark 9: 30-37

The Servant of All

Jesus and the disciples were returning to Capernaum. Darkening rain clouds in the angry sky matched their dark moods. The disciples had fallen behind the faster-paced Jesus, walking and talking in groups of two or three. Up ahead, Jesus seemed cloaked in disappointment as he walked alone.

A little while earlier the disciples heard Jesus tell them the disturbing words:

"The Son of Man is going to be delivered into the hands of men who will put him to death; three days after his death he will rise."

This pronouncement launched a flurry of exasperating questions which served to separate them from Jesus. The disciples failed to understand what Jesus told them, and seeing his exasperation with them, they fell behind, clumping together in little discussion groups. No one wanted to ask Jesus what he really meant by such improbable words. They were all going to be part of the new kingdom.

Jesus had momentarily given up. Things hadn't been going well. He thought about his death, the death he had just foretold. He thought about how he would have to let them take him from this world. He would no longer walk in these hills and enjoy the familiar countryside.

Nearing Capernaum he overheard some of the disciples arguing about what their positions would be in the kingdom to come. Such dreams were understandable. People were born into their station in life and there was almost no chance to improve on it. A fisherman would always be a fisherman. The poor, shepherds and slaves remained in their status. The disciples thought that Jesus was offering them a new order, a new kingdom. They would no longer be fishermen, they would be the new aristocracy.

Back in Peter's house Jesus said to them: "What were you discussing on the way home?"

No one answered because they knew that he must have heard them. Jesus sat down and motioned for them to join him.

One of Peter's young nephews, a boy about four years of age, suddenly burst into the room. He stopped, surprised at all the strangers. Then he recog-

nized Jesus and came up to him. Jesus hugged the boy who reached up to explore Jesus' beard. Gently taking the boy's hand, Jesus said to his disciples: "If anyone of you wishes to rank first, he must remain the last one of all and be the servant of all."

Then looking at the young boy, Jesus continued: "Whoever welcomes a child such as this for my sake, welcomes me. And whoever welcomes me welcomes, not me, but him who sent me."

Some of the disciples smiled in agreement as they began to understood Jesus' example. Children were the least of society, powerless, dependent on others and without rank.

To be first the disciples would have to remain last, even after children. They would have to be the servants of all.

☦

Jesus seems to be describing Mother Teresa! She was the servant of all. She was the servant of the lowest and least. Because of that she was honored and exalted by an applauding world.

26th Sunday in Ordinary Time
Mark 9: 39-43; 45; 47-48

All God's good works

The man fell over backwards, falling stiffly. He slammed into the ground so hard that dust exploded out from under him. His left leg began to kick wildly, as if he was trying to shake off an evil spirit that had slithered from the ground and seized it. His whole body began to convulse while groaning sounds and drool came from his mouth.

A wild-eyed magician jumped forward from the crowd that was gathering.. He circled the fallen man like a predator and suddenly raised his hands to the sky, shouting in a raspy voice:

"I command you evil spirits to depart... to come out of this man's body. By the power of Jesus of Nazareth, I call you out!"

Just then the man on the ground stopped seizing and was calm. It was a miracle! Like a wink of sunlight through the clouds, an exultation flashed over the exorcist's face revealing the beginnings of a smile. Quickly, he struggled to maintain his stern composure. The exorcist then proudly walked away, holding his head high.

Outraged, the disciple John called after him, "Magician, by what authority do you use the name of Jesus? I am one of his disciples and you are not one of our group!"

The demon-expeller turned back, snarling at John: "You have seen my power at work. Be silent!" The fallen man was now getting up, sleepily brushing off his clothes.

Later that day, John told Jesus about the incident, "I was wishing that I had tried to stop this magician from using your name."

Jesus said: "Do not try to stop him. No man who performs a miracle using my name can at once speak ill of me. Anyone who is not against us is with us. Any one who gives you a drink of water because you belong to Christ will not, I assure you, go without his reward. But, it would be better if anyone who leads astray one of these simple believers were to be plunged in the sea with a great millstone fastened around his neck."

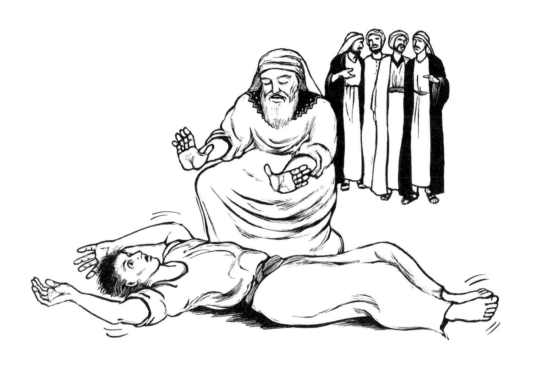

✝

    While this apparent exorcism may have been nothing more than merely allowing time for an epileptic seizure to run its course, those who witnessed it saw a magical power done in the name of Jesus by an exorcist who was not an official disciple. Jesus' response is a lesson in appreciating that good works come in many shapes and sizes.

    In less ecumenical days than we now enjoy, many Catholics did not see the openness of God's love for all of his people—be they Muslim, Protestant or Buddhist. As President Lincoln once said: we shouldn't worry if God is on our side, more important we should ask ourselves the question: 'are we on God's side?'

27th Sunday in Ordinary Time
Mark 10: 2-16

Let the little children come to me!

J esus and the disciples started early—it was a ten mile walk to the next village. They were avoiding the hot mid-day sun, traveling in the relatively cooler morning. They followed the main road north along the shores of the Sea of Galilee. After several hours of steady walking they could finally scc their destination. It was a dark cluster of houses beneath a canopy of big shade trees. An arm of land encircled the small bay of the fishing village. A few boats were hauled up on the gravel beach.

Jesus noticed people were running from the village toward him. As they drew closer he saw that they were children, more than a dozen. Jesus smiled over at Peter, walking by his side.

"Looks like we have a greeting party coming our way," he said.

"Word travels fast," Peter responded.

As Jesus entered the main street of the village he was waist-deep in children who were escorting him. Seeing that the famous healer was already here, shopkeepers left their stalls and joined the growing crowd. Up ahead a woman poured out a bowl of water and offered it to Jesus. He smiled his thanks at her and quickly lifted the cool water to his lips, drinking deeply. As he tilted his head back to drink it all, some ran over the side and onto his beard. The droplets fell to the gray sand at Jesus' feet. "Oh, thank you. I really needed that," Jesus said to the water woman. She smiled back and lowered her gaze in respect.

Jesus saw a good place to sit in the shade of one of the big trees and lowered himself to the ground, cross-legged. Immediately the children crowded in around him. Mothers with children in their arms edged closer. Soon Jesus was overwhelmed by the crowd.

Peter rose to his feet, holding up the palms of his hands. "Step back!" he bellowed. "Give us some room. we have been walking all morning. We need some moments to rest."

The faces of the children and the mothers darkened as they stepped back. Peter moved between the crowd and Jesus, cutting a path with his bold stride and stern glare.

Then Jesus rose to his feet, saying softly, "No, Peter." He waved his scolding finger at Peter and the other disciples. "No, no, no." Peter stopped where he was and looked questioningly at Jesus. He had only been trying to help. Jesus looked back with gentleness. "It's alright.," he said. Then he moved back to his place and sat down. Looking up at them he smiled broadly. "Now, let the little children come to me. It is to just such as these that the Kingdom of God belongs."

A tide of children moved back to Jesus and he reached out, putting his arms about them and blessing them with his caressing hands.

✝

In the first part of this Sunday's gospel reading, Jesus condemns divorce and adultery and affirms the sanctity of marriage. He says the union of man and wife, make the two one flesh and that God has joined them. In the second part of the gospel we hear about the children and how Jesus blessed them and loved them. Both stories connect because the children become one with their parents in the bonds of family. When man and woman put their marriage asunder, it tears the children asunder as well. It is this separation that Jesus denounces when he calls the little children back into his embrace.

28th Sunday in Ordinary Time
Mark 10: 17-30

Sell what you have and give to the poor...

Jesus looked down at the well-dressed man kneeling in the mud before him. The man's knees were grinding the finely-woven fabric of his robe into the still soft mud from yesterday's rain. Such homage from a man of wealth was an incredible act of respect.

"What must I do?" he asked of Jesus.

The man was still breathing heavily from having run to catch up with Jesus and the disciples as they were leaving the town. As he looked up at Jesus there was urgency and sincerity in his eyes.

Jesus knelt down by him and put both of his hands on the man's shoulders. Looking lovingly in the man's eyes, Jesus gave his answer.

"You lack one thing. Go and sell what you have, and give to the poor, and you will have treasure in heaven; and come, follow me."

In the flat light from the overcast sky, the man's face darkened as he realized he would not be able to do that. He had spent a lifetime acquiring property, a beautiful home and many slaves to work for him. He owned several business enterprises. He even had a great bag filled with gold and silver coins which he had secretly buried underneath a floor stone in his bedroom.

The rich man knew he could not leave everything and follow Jesus. His several businesses needed his attention. There were shipments due in from Antioch. His collections, everything else he owned were just too wonderful to give away. It was out of the question.

Jesus, seeing the man's distress, rose to his feet and began to move on. The rich man stood helplessly, his hands and knees black with mud. Jesus stopped and turned back, looking in silence at the sorrowful figure so weighted down by his possessions. It was a last invitation to be one of the Apostles and to experience the boundless treasure of heaven. The man looked longingly back at Jesus. His eyes were wet with emotion. Then he turned his back on Jesus and slowly walked toward the town.

As they resumed their walk, Jesus said to the disciples around him: "How

hard it will be for those who have riches to enter the kingdom of God."

As Peter walked by Jesus' side he remembered the one silver coin that he had hidden in the lining of his sack. The coin grew heavier in Peter's heart as he began to think about giving it away.

☩

We need to possess and use worldly goods. Jesus does not condemn this. He simply uses this exceptional example of the rich man to point out the danger of being overly-attached to our possessions.

We need to see the bigger picture. Our lives and everything on earth, are only temporary. The lasting value is in the treasure of heaven which has been promised to us.

We are invited to travel light so that we can help others with their burdens. Part of the discipline of traveling light is to practice giving away some of the wealth we have.

29th Sunday in Ordinary Time
Mark 10-35-45

The Sons of Thunder

It was almost dark. The skewered fish were roasting over the fire. Jesus sat staring out at the last light on the lake. He was realizing that this would be the last time he would ever be here at the lake like this.

Jesus remembered the spring afternoon when he had called Peter and his brother Andrew to follow him. Then, later, the two sons of Zebedee, James and John, who jumped off the family fishing boat, leaving their father behind.

From across the fire, Jesus could see James and his younger brother John; he couldn't hear their voices, but he knew they were talking about him.

"When we get to Jerusalem," James was saying, "Jesus will take power. He will take over everything."

John asked, "How can it happen?"

"He is the Messiah, don't ask how!" James snapped back at his brother. "He will throw out the Romans and establish his kingdom with the power of God!"

"And he will need us at his right hand too," John said.

James smiled. "We'll have to put it to him."

In the morning, many from the villages came to see Jesus and the disciples before they left Galilee. The mother of James and John came out of the crowd to find her boys. She knew that Jesus was going to Jerusalem where they said he would become a king. Bowing before the future king she begged, "Promise me these two sons of mine will sit at your right hand and your left hand when you are king."

Jesus saw in her the boldness that had been reborn in James and John. He smiled, remembering that he nicknamed them "Sons of Thunder" after the time they had been ready to ask the heavens to send fire down upon the unfriendly Samaritans.

Starting out on the road for Jerusalem, Jesus took the lead. The others followed. It was tradition that the teacher would walk first. Like warriors on the eve of battle, there was a growing anxiety among the disciples as they began to worry about facing the capitol city and the might of Rome.

Jesus was concerned about his twelve disciples' lack of understanding

about what he meant by kingdom. During a rest, Jesus took them aside and explained that in Jerusalem he would be handed over to the authorities who would condemn him and put him to death, but that he would rise to life.

Instead of understanding, when they resumed walking again, James and John caught up with Jesus and fell into step beside him. James presented him with the challenge: "Teacher we want you to do for us whatever we ask of you."

Jesus asked: "What do you want me to do for you?"

"Grant us," James pleaded, "to sit, one at your right hand and one at your left, when you come into your glory."

Jesus told them they did not know what they were asking and described the trials ahead of them. Soon the other ten disciples were protesting as they began to squabble like hungry animals over the scraps of imagined future power.

Jesus ended it all when he patiently explained again: "The Son of man came not to be served, but to serve, and to give his life as a ransom for many."

☩

How hard it is for people to separate today's bread from tomorrow's promise. Perhaps many of us have prayed to be served with special treatment. Jesus asks us to follow his example of sacrifice—not to be served but to serve. To be great we must become servants. To become great we must be a slave to all.

30th Sunday in Ordinary Time
Mark 10: 46-52

Your faith
has healed you

Bartimaeus sat in the darkness feeling the sun's warmth on his face. He smelled bread baking. The scent drifted in the stillness of the morning air and Bartimaeus knew it was almost nine o'clock. The first batch of bread was always done by then. Even though he was blind, Bartimaeus measured the routine of Jericho by its sounds and scents.

Today's routine was going to be different because Jesus and his disciples were passing through on their way up to Bethany. The stories of Jesus' healing and legends about his miracles always drew great crowds. It had drawn Bartimaeus as well because he knew Jesus had the power to restore his sight. He only had to somehow find him.

Bartimaeus positioned himself on the Bethany road a short distance outside Jericho. He sat down on the ground and listened for the sound of a crowd. He would wait there until Jesus passed by. An hour slowly passed. Bartimaeus listened. Then, from the direction of Jericho, he heard people coming. Bartimaeus couldn't know where Jesus was going to be in the crowd or exactly when he would be passing by, so as soon as the crunch of feet was clear he began to cry out in a loud voice: "Jesus, Son of David, have pity on me."

He kept repeating it, bellowing his plea as loud as he could. Bartimaeus heard the crowd passing by and was afraid Jesus had already gone by too. Desperately, he began to shout all the louder.

"Shut-up, blind man!" someone yelled at him. Bartimaeus screamed all the louder.

Jesus heard the noise and stopped, turning to one of the disciples. "Call him over," Jesus said.

Two of the disciples went to the roadside and each took the blind man by an arm. At first Bartimaeus struggled to get away, thinking they were the men who had told him to shut up.

"Hey, hey, its okay, you have nothing to fear. Get up. Jesus is calling you." they said. The disciples helped Bartimaeus to his feet and escorted him through

the crowd to stand before Jesus.

"What do you want?" Jesus asked.

"I want to see."

"Be on your way, your faith has healed you," Jesus announced.

Light burst upon Bartimaeus like an explosion. Rivers of vivid colors flowed into his eyes. It was so intense that he had to shield his eyes from the brilliance which slowly softened into the white-robed shape of a man standing before him.

Bartimaeus began to cry and through his tears he saw Jesus turn his back on him and begin to walk way.

Forgetting his cloak at the roadside, Bartimaeus began to follow, joining the crowds that were moving up into the mountains toward Bethany and in a few days, Jerusalem.

✝

Jesus still does miracles. Each of us has been given sight to see beyond the spectrum of this earth and this time. When we are able to see the vision of Jesus before us, we, like Bartimaeus are flooded with light and rivers of joyous color course through our being. All we need to do is to place ourselves before Jesus and with the faith that healed Bartimaeus, open our eyes, open our ears, and open our hearts.

31st Sunday in Ordinary Time
Mark 12: 28-34

No greater commandment

Driven by warm wind, the rain slanted down, coating the courtyard stones with a glossy varnish. Vendors ducked in under their tent cloths trying to keep themselves and their wares dry.

The steps leading up to the Temple had become broad waterfalls from the downpour. Standing with their backs to the wall of the Great Temple, Jesus and Peter found some protection from the Spring squall.

Jesus looked out over the city, muted by the white veil of rain. There were only a few days left. The sight of Roman soldiers moving on the parapets of Fortress Antonia re-awakened a dark shadow of Roman brutality. It clutched at him as his life's images of violence and cruelty lashed across his mind.

Jesus breathed deeply, letting the cool, rain-filled air invigorate him. The fresh smell of the rain made him smile again.

Peter also seemed exhilarated by the rain. Jesus looked into the big fisherman's eyes. They were distant, perhaps remembering another drenching downpour he'd experienced out on the lake.

They stood awhile longer looking at wet Jerusalem. Then Jesus said, "Looks like this rain is going to keep up. Let's go inside."

The two hurried under the raindrops to the entrance of the sanctuary. Inside, they found a group of men busy in conversation. Among them were Temple rabbis arguing about points of the Jewish law. Jesus and Peter, glad to be inside, sat nearby to listen to the debate.

The rabbi who was talking recognized Jesus and looked uneasily at him, remembering him as the one who drove the moneychangers and sellers out of the temple. He continued, trying to ignore Jesus, but his glances made the others curious. They too turned to see the two newcomers to the sanctuary.

One of the scribes called over to Jesus, inviting him to join in the debate: "Which commandment is the first of all?"

Jesus quoted from memory the words of Deuteronomy: "Hear O Israel, the Lord is our God alone..." Many in his hearing recognized the words which exhorted them to love their One God with all their strength.

The scribe pressed for more, nodding his head for Jesus to continue. From

the Scroll of Leviticus Jesus quoted the words: "You shall love your neighbor as yourself."

Jesus added, "There is no commandment greater than these."

The scribe began to smile in understanding. All the other commandments of God clearly flowed from these.

Jesus reflected on how he would truly love those who soon would torture and kill him.

"There is no commandment greater than this!" Peter said, not realizing he was underscoring Jesus' thoughts.

The sound of the rain diminished summoning Jesus and Peter to the entrance of the Temple. A last few drops fell from the swiftly scudding clouds. They started down the steps and Jesus felt a warmth on his back. Turning, he saw a golden burst of sunlight find its way out of the thinning clouds. The light seemed to caress him. Jesus sighed and hurried down the steps after Peter.

✝

Truly there is no greater commandment than to love God with all our heart, soul and strength. It is in this love of God that we find the ability to love our neighbors as ourselves. This is where we find the kingdom of God and our place in it.

32nd Sunday in Ordinary Time
Mark 12: 41-44

She gave
all that she had

The great Temple of Jerusalem was perched on the highest land in the city. From the Temple one could look out across the Kidron Valley to the Mount of Olives. In the other direction were the banners of Herod's Palace. To the north the parapets of Antonia Fortress were manned by Roman Centurions. Looking south over the royal portico was the Hinnom Valley, Golgotha and in the far distance the high hills which contained the village of Bethlehem.

The entrance to the Temple was flanked by two great columns made of bronze. The columns soared 40 feet into the air and were named Jachin and Boaz. Passing between them, Jesus walked into the sanctuary and looked toward the steps that continued higher to an inner room, the holy of holies, where the Ark of the Covenant had been kept.

Jesus took a seat opposite the treasury and looked at the thick walls and counted 13 bronze chests for the deposit of offerings. The tops of the chests were flared like hungry trumpets ready to swallow as much as people would give.

The Temple was extravagantly decorated. Herod's wealth and a prosperous Jerusalem supported this royal center of religion. Wealthy men in fine clothes made generous contributions, some even lifting up their bright gold and silver offering so that everyone could see their generosity. Lavishly robed rabbis and temple priests pompously paraded in the busy temple taking little note of the small woman who was shuffling into the Court of the Women. Jesus watched her with interest. She was hunched over with the weight of many years. Her shabby clothes were a stark contrast to the elegant garments of the merchants and temple officials gliding by. She approached one of the bronze offering chests and began to search through in her cloth bag. She brought out a dull coin, a mite, the least denomination. With her blotchy hand shaking, she reached up and dropped the coin over the edge of the trumpet-mouth. There was no sound as it disappeared. She then dug into the bag again and found her last coin.

Her face was stoic and full of faith as she let that coin slip from her fingers into the gaping chest. She turned away and began to shuffle slowly out of the temple. Jesus was greatly moved by this. He sat motionless, watching her small figure move into the brighter light outside the Temple.

✝

The teachings of Jesus show us again and again that we can't buy our way or power our way into paradise. We must truly believe and have the simple faith of the widow who gave her last coins. We must follow the great commandments to love one another. We must follow the servant example of Jesus who washed the feet of his disciples.

33rd Sunday in Ordinary Time
Mark 13: 24-32

No one knows the day and the hour

It had been four years since the Resurrection of the Lord and a small group of the followers of Jesus were meeting together to share a meal and retell the story. Mark was hosting the evening at his home in Jerusalem. The Disciple Peter was the guest of honor.

Peter finished his wine and placed his cup back on the table. Then he began to remember. "Jesus told us that after trials of every sort the sun will be darkened, the moon will not shed its light, stars will fall out of the skies, and the heavenly hosts will be shaken."

The fearsome imagery played across their minds. Peter continued: "Jesus said we will see the Son of Man coming in the clouds with great power and glory. He will dispatch his messengers and assemble his chosen from the four winds, from the farthest bounds of the earth and sky.

Mark looked up from taking notes. "When is this to happen, Peter?" Some of the others in the room had heard Peter tell this story before and knew he was coming to the fig tree answer.

Peter told them about how the seasons can be foretold by the fig tree. Then he said: "But Jesus told us as to the exact day and hour, no one knows it. Neither the angels in heaven nor even the Son, but only the Father."

Mark wrote it down. When he looked up he said to everyone in the room. "That's right. In the last days Jesus did not know the exact day or the hour of his crucifixion. They could have held him until after the Passover." The group murmured agreement.

Peter added his final thoughts: "None of us knows when our time will come. But, we must be prepared." Peter was going to tell Jesus' parable story about the ten bridesmaids, but Mark was still busy writing things down. The others seemed to have enough to think about. They were already talking among themselves about the coming of the Lord.

✟

    Jesus left us with a clear picture that this universe will one day come to an end. We will not know the exact day or hour, but we know it will happen. And just as surely, our lives will end. No matter how many years we have lived, all too soon we find that our life is over. Jesus paints these word pictures and tells us these things so that we can be prepared to meet him when he comes. That is why, after saying the Our Father at each Mass, we pray: "Deliver us, Lord, from every evil, and grant us peace in our day. In your mercy keep us free from sin and protect us from all anxiety as we wait in joyful hope for the coming of our Savior, Jesus Christ."

Christ the King
John 18: 33-37

My kingdom is not of this world

Pontius Pilate stepped up onto the stone platform and slowly settled himself in the judgment seat. He crossed his legs and rested himself against the chair's left arm. He sat in silence for several minutes as he studied the prisoner before him. The man was bruised and bloody from the beatings. He seemed beyond exhaustion and could barely stand.

"Are you the King of the Jews?" Pilate asked.

Jesus lifted his bruised head to answer. His speech came slowly, slurred through his swollen, cracked lips. Jesus' mouth was dry. All through the long night they had given him no water. Only the taste of blood had quenched his nagging thirst.

Jesus boldly answered Pilate by turning the question back to him: "Are you saying this on your own, or have others been telling you about me?"

Pilate sat on the edge of the chair and put both feet on the platform. "I am no Jew! It is your own people and the chief priests who have handed you over to me. What have you done?"

Jesus staggered to the right, caught his balance and then continued to speak: "My kingdom does not belong to this world. If my kingdom were of this world my subjects would be fighting to save me from being handed over to the Jews."

Pilate seemed to be listening carefully. Jesus locked eyes with him. "As it is," Jesus paused, "my kingdom is not here."

Pilate leaned forward, "So then you are a king?"

"It is you who say I am a king," Jesus protested through his pain.

Pilate made no response, ignoring the way Jesus was turning his words back against him.

Talking had opened the crusty cuts in his swollen lips and Jesus could again taste blood. Pain was burning everywhere in his body.

Grimly he found the strength to finish: "The reason I was born, the rea-

son why I came into the world, is to testify to the truth. Anyone committed to the truth hears my voice."

✝

If we consider ourselves members of God's kingdom here on earth, we must ask ourselves if Christ is really king in our lives? Jesus told Pilate that he came into the world to testify to the truths about God and man. Each of us must, in our own time, discover that truth for ourselves. We then must believe the truth, live out that truth and share the truth of love with one another. In that way the bearer of truth, Jesus Christ, becomes the king of our lives.

The Gospel Stories of Jesus is available on a CD Rom

To facilitate the insertion of each weekly Gospel story into your church Sunday bulletin, or other program, this book has been downloaded onto a CD.

The text is in Microsoft Word and the accompanying illustration is stored as a jpeg. This will enable you to flow the text into your particular format. You can size the illustration to fit your space.

Insert the CD in your computer, scroll to the current week and highlight the story. Then just copy and paste. The same procedure applies for the illustration.

Here's how to order the CD version:

To order by mail

Send your check for $9.95 to
  The Gospel Stories of Jesus
  32026 Trevor Avenue
  Hayward, California 94544

To order by phone

  call Deacon Dick Folger direct
  at **510-475-7669**.

If you wish to order via the internet, just e-mail

  dickfolger@aol.com
  Please include the following information:
  Ship to address
  Authorization to charge your credit card for $9.95.
  Include credit card number and expiration.

Your postage paid order will be sent to you by U.S. Mail.